Excel
Basics to Advanced

Design Robust Spreadsheet Applications Powered with Formatting, Advanced Calculations, Charts, Pivot Tables, and Macros.

Chandraish Sinha

www.ohiocomputeracademy.com

Legal Notes

First Edition.
ISBN: 978-0-9992449-6-8

Dedicated to

Ishie
My daughter, who excels in every little thing she does…

About the Author

Chandraish Sinha is the Founder/President of Ohio Computer Academy, a company dedicated to IT education.

An IT training enthusiast, Chandraish resonates with his company's slogan - Inspire, Educate and Evolve. He is a Business Intelligence learner and explorer, with a strong background in implementing multiple large and medium-scale BI solutions.

Throughout his 22-year career, Chandraish has worked with a variety of Business Intelligence and dashboarding applications, such as Tableau, Power BI, Qlik View, Qlik Sense, IBM Cognos, Business Objects, and Actuate. His passion for data leads him to explore applications that provide better data insights.

Chandraish is an accomplished author with multiple published books on various topics. To view his Amazon author profile, visit amazon.com/author/ chandraishsinha.

He actively maintains his blogs, where he regularly shares insights and knowledge on applications such as MS Excel, Tableau, Power BI, and QlikView. Readers can find his blogs at the following links:

- https://ohiocomputeracademy.com/category/msexcel/
- https://ohiocomputeracademy.com/category/tableau/
- https://ohiocomputeracademy.com/category/power-bi/
- https://www.learntableaupublic.com/
- https://www.learnallbi.com/

Connect with him on LinkedIn:
www.linkedin.com/in/chandraishsinha

Other books by the author:

1. Dashboarding with Tableau
2. Mastering Power BI
3. Tableau Unlimited
4. Implementing Tableau Server
5. Tableau 10 for Beginners
6. Tableau Dashboards: Step by Step guide to developing visualizations in Tableau 9.2
7. Tableau Questions & Answers: Guide to Tableau concepts and FAQs
8. QlikView Essentials
9. QlikView Questions and Answers: Guide to QlikView and FAQs
10. How to be a Successful IT Professional in the USA: A Checklist and Easy Guide to Success

Acknowledgement

My earnest thanks to all my readers who have supported my books so far and inspired me to pursue further. I personally read all their reviews and feedback.

I am grateful to the entire Microsoft community at large for creating numerous blogs, videos, and other content. They provide immense learning and exploring opportunities.

I extend my sincere thanks to my students for asking challenging questions and encouraging me to learn more.

Book writing involves the effort of many people, and I am thankful to all of them for providing the necessary assistance.

Preface

Microsoft Excel is the popular application due to its versatile features and capabilities. Its useful features, data manipulation capabilities, PivotTables, and powerful functions empower users to efficiently organize, analyze, and present data in various formats.

Having worked in different Business Intelligence applications, including Tableau, Power BI, and Qlik, I've come to realize that Excel is the building block for BI and data analysis. In fact, these applications heavily rely on Excel. Additionally, organizations use Excel to test the reports and dashboards designed in these applications.

Excel is essential for anyone starting a career in Information Technology, as it forms the basis of databases and helps in understanding how functions work in calculations.

This book introduces readers to the basics and gradually advances to deeper concepts. A sincere attempt has been made to cover all the aspects of MS Excel from start to finish.

The technique I have followed in this book is to explain the concept followed by a hands-on exercise. All the data and solution files are provided. Readers can follow the steps provided in the book and create their own spreadsheets.

This book can be used with any version of Excel. The basic workings of Excel have not changed over the years, but new features get added with the newer versions.

The goal of this book is to provide readers with a comprehensive and practical resource that will not only improve their Excel skills but also empower them to leverage Excel as a valuable tool in personal and professional endeavors. I have taken care to explain concepts in a clear and straightforward manner, making this book suitable for both self-study and as a reference guide.

Over the 11 chapters in this book, you will learn the following:

Chapter 1 covers the basics of MS Excel and explains all the important terminologies. It assists in installing the application and provides detail explanations of the ribbon and other functionalities such as Sorting, Filtering, Printing and more.

Chapter 2 explains how to format data in an Excel spreadsheet. It also covers conditional formatting in Excel.

Chapter 3 Introduces the readers to the formulas and calculations. It also explains the concept of different types of cell references and their usefulness in creating calculations.

Chapter 4 deals with Logical functions and how they are used in performing logical tests using IF, AND, and OR functions.

Chapter 5 discusses Text functions in Excel and how to perform string manipulation using functions like LEFT, RIGHT, LEN, CONCAT, and more.

Chapter 6 explains DateTime functions in Excel. It starts with how dates are represented in Excel and how to use different date functions.

Chapter 7 takes a deep dive into Mathematical functions such as COUNT, SUM, SUMIFS, and more.

Chapter 8 covers in detail the Lookup and Reference functions such as VLOOKUP, LOOKUP, INDEX, and MATCH.

Chapter 9 explains Pivot tables and charts. Pivot tables are essential for aggregating and analyzing data, and charts are used to present data visually.

Chapter 10 covers Excel tables, which provide added functionality on the range of cells. It explains how to create an Excel table and use to them to analyze the data.

Chapter 11 introduces Macros in Excel, which are used to automate the repetitive tasks. The chapter explains how to record and run a Macro.

How to use this book:

The book comes with enclosed datasets providing practice workbooks and solution workbooks. The practice workbooks are located in the *Data/ Practice* folder, and the solution workbooks are available in the *Data/Solutions* folder. Download the *Data* folder to access these files.

Readers are encouraged to use the practice workbooks and perform the exercises by following the steps provided in the book. Readers can refer to the solutions for the output.

Downloading the code

Please follow the link given below to download the *Data files*. The folder contains both practice and solution files:

https://ohiocomputeracademy.com/ms-excel-basics-to-advanced/

Password: MS@Excel

Errata

In creating this work, any unforeseen errors might have occurred. If any readers encounter difficulties due to processing errors, please write to us at:

hello@ohiocomputeracademy.com

with subject line: ***Errata Excel Basics to Advanced***

Your support, suggestions, and feedbacks are highly appreciated by the Author.

He personally reads and responds to all messages.

Table of Contents

Chapter 1
MS Excel Fundamentals

MS Excel or Microsoft Excel is a popular spreadsheet application that empowers users to organize, analyze, and manipulate data efficiently. This chapter will begin by exploring the user interface, including ribbon, Worksheets, and Cells. Additionally, it will cover data entry and demonstrate how to perform filtering and sorting operations.

The following topics will be discussed in this chapter:

- Introducing MS Excel
- Installation
- Understanding the ribbon
- Understanding the workbook
- Creating your first Excel workbook
- Freeze Pane
- Sorting
- Filtering the data
- Task bar
- Printing in Excel

Introducing MS Excel

MS Excel stands for Microsoft Excel, is a spreadsheet program developed by Microsoft Corporation. It is a part of the MS Office suite of business applications and enables users to format, organize, and perform calculations on data in a spreadsheet format. Excel was first launched in 1985.

Importance of MS Excel

MS Excel is utilized by organizations in a variety of ways. Some of the usages of MS excel include:

- Data storage: MS Excel's vast grid allows for storing large amounts of data, making it ideal for data storage purposes.
- Data validation: The built-in functionalities in MS Excel facilitate quick and efficient data validation.
- Data analysis: Excel's ability to generate reports and charts makes it valuable for data analysis tasks.
- Creating wireframes: Excel can be utilized to create wireframes for website designs and dashboard layouts.
- Day-to-day tasks: MS Excel is handy for various day-to-day tasks like creating attendance reports, accounting, and time management.
- Basis for learning other applications: Proficiency in MS Excel can serve as a foundation for learning other tools and applications, including database management and reporting platforms like Tableau and Power BI.

MS Excel is a powerful and versatile spreadsheet application that plays a crucial role in various organizations and industries. Moreover, MS Excel serves as a stepping stone for learning more advanced applications and tools, making it an essential skill in today's data-driven world.

MS Excel Terminology

A good knowledge of the terminology and keywords used in MS Excel are essential in order to master the application. Some common terms are listed in Table 1.1 MS Excel Terminology, below.

Table:1.1 MS Excel Terminology.

Terminology	Description
Workbook	A design file created in Excel is called a Workbook. One workbook can contain multiple worksheets.
Worksheet	An individual spreadsheet in a workbook.
XLS/XLSX	The commonly used extensions of an Excel file are XLS/XLSX. XLS is the default file format from Excel 97-2003, and XLSX is the default format for Excel 2007 and later.
Data	Data entered on a spreadsheet can be a number, text, or an image.
Rows/Columns	The data in a worksheet is stored in row and column format. Rows are horizontal, and columns are vertical.
Cell	The data is entered/stored in a cell, which is an intersection of a row and column.
Cell reference /address	It is a combination of row (number) and column (letter) that identifies the position of a cell on a spreadsheet.
Formula	Uses the built-in functions in Excel and perform computations such mathematical, string, logical, etc.
Pivot table	A Pivot table is used to summarize the data present in the spreadsheet.
Pivot charts	The graphical representation of the summarized data is done using charts.
Sort	Arranging the data based on the value or the data type.
Filter	A Filter is used to display the data based on the specified criteria.
Macro	A Macro is a series of recorded or manually written commands that automate repetitive tasks within Excel.

Understanding the key terminology and concepts in MS Excel is crucial for effectively using the application. Having a grasp of these fundamental Excel terms provides a solid foundation for working with spreadsheets.

Installation

Installation of MS-Excel is required to perform the exercises provided in this book. MS Excel is part of MS Office applications, these applications come in two flavors:

- MS Office 365: It is a subscription-based version that offers access to the latest features and updates, along with cloud-based storage and collaboration options.
- MS Office stand-alone: It is a one-time purchase version that provides a fixed set of features and does not receive regular updates like Office 365.

For the exercises in this book, readers can use either version of MS Office, but having MS Excel installed is necessary to follow along and practice the concepts explained throughout the chapters. The installation steps for both are the same.

Installation of Office 365

Below are the steps to install Office 365:

1. Open any internet browser and go to www.office.com. Click on *Sign in* located in the top-right corner. If you don't have an account, create a new one.
2. On the Microsoft 365 Home page, click on *Install Office*. This will start the download and installation process for Microsoft 365 on your machine.

Note: By default, a 64-bit version of the app will be installed unless Microsoft 365 detects a 32-bit version already installed. In that case, the 32-bit version will be installed.

3. Depending on the browser used to download Office 365, select *Run* (in Microsoft edge or Internet explorer), *Setup* (in chrome), or *Save File* (in Firefox).
4. On the prompt *Do you want to allow this app to make changes to your device*, select *Yes.* This will start the installation process.
5. Once the installation is complete, a message will be displayed on the screen, "You're all set! Office is installed now." An animation will be played to show where to find Microsoft 365 applications on the computer.
6. Select *Close.*
7. To open Microsoft 365 apps, select the *Start* button on your machine and type the name of the app, such as *Excel.*
8. When the app opens, accept the license agreement.

Note: To launch MS Excel on the machine, click on the Windows button and type *Excel.*

Understanding the ribbon

The Microsoft Excel ribbon enables users to execute commands to perform desired tasks. It is divided into the following sections:

- Tabs. The Ribbon consists of various tabs such as File, Home, Insert, etc.
- Groups. Each tab contains multiple Groups which are sets of related commands.
- Action buttons. Groups contain action buttons/icons to execute a command.
- More Group options. A small downward arrow at the bottom right of each group launches more options provided in the group.

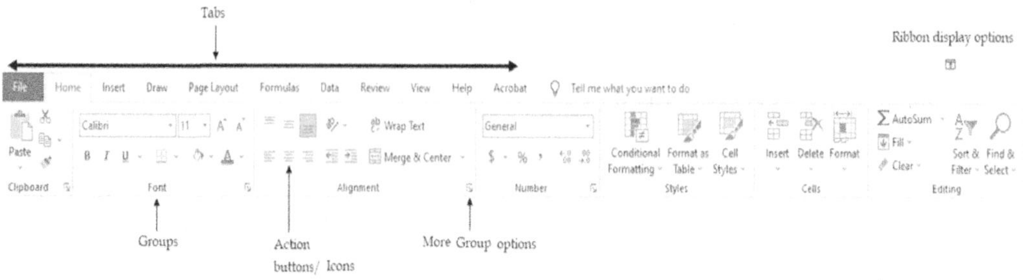

Figure 1.1: MS Excel Ribbon.

The options available on the ribbon are explained in Table 1.1, providing details of each option as displayed in Figure 1.1.

Table:1.1 MS Excel Ribbon options.

Ribbon Option	**Description**
Tabs	MS Excel ribbon consists of tabs such as File, Home, Insert, Draw, Page Layout, Formulas, Data, Review, View, Help, and Acrobat.
Groups	Each tab consists of Groups. For example, the *Home* tab consists of Groups such as Font, Alignment, Number, etc.
Action buttons/Icons	Each Group consists of buttons and icons, such B for Bold, I for Italics, icons for colors, alignment, etc.
More Group Options	The downward arrow on a group displays more options available in that group.
Ribbon display options	The ribbon also has an icon displayed on the top-right that provides the option to show/hide the ribbon.

Ribbon Tabs

The Excel ribbon tabs are customizable. Tabs can be shown or hidden from the options in the File menu. The ribbon commonly consists of the following tabs:

File
The File tab provides options for opening, saving the workbook, and printing. It also provides the More/Options command, which can be used to customize the ribbon and other features of the workbook.

Home
The Home tab contains the most frequently used commands, such as formatting, alignment, and styles, etc.

Insert
The insert tab is used for adding various objects to the sheet. This tab can be used to add Pivot tables, charts, illustrations, links, etc.

Draw
The draw tab provides options to draw on the screen with the digital pen, mouse or finger. If this tab is not present on the ribbon, it can be added from File > More > Options.

Page Layout
Use the Page Layout tab to manage the appearance of the worksheet. This includes Themes, Page Setup, and other formatting options related to the layout of the printed page.

Formulas
The Formulas tab includes all the functions used in Excel formulas. It provides access to a wide range of mathematical, statistical, logical, and text functions that enable powerful data calculations and analysis.

Data

The Data tab helps in managing the data in the current worksheet and provides tools to connect to external data sources as well. It includes features for sorting, filtering, data validation, data import, and data analysis.

Review

The Review tab contains commands that help in reviewing the document by performing spell checks, adding comments, and tracking changes. It also includes options for protecting the worksheet and managing workbook security.

View

The View tab helps in viewing the data in the worksheet in a desired way. It contains commands for different views, freeze panes, and adjusting the zoom level for better visibility.

Help

The Help tab offers options for accessing help and support on MS Excel, including accessing the Help documentation and getting assistance from Microsoft's support resources.

Acrobat

The Acrobat tab contains commands to convert worksheets in a workbook into a PDF document. This tab requires Acrobat to be installed on the machine, and the PDF Add-in needs to be enabled. The PDF add-in can be enabled by navigating to File > Options > Add-ins and selecting the PDF add-in from the list of available add-ins.

Ribbon Tab Shortcuts

The ribbon tables can be accessed through keyboard shortcuts, which are combinations of the ALT and other keys on the keyboard.

Press the ALT key to display the ribbon shortcuts, also known as *Key Tips*. These Key Tips are the small images of letters displayed next to the tabs and options. Combine these Key Tips letters with the ALT key to create the shortcuts. For example, ALT + F will display the File menu.

The Table 1.2 provides some of the ribbon shortcuts.

Table:1.2 Ribbon shortcuts.

Ribbon shortcut	**Description**
ALT + F	Open the File Menu
ALT + H	Open the Home tab
ALT + N	Open the Insert tab
ALT + P	Open the Page Layout tab
ALT + M	Open the Formulas Tab
ALT + A	Open the Data Tab
ALT + R	Open the Review tab
ALT + W	Open the View tab
ALT + Y +2	Open the Design tab
ALT + J +1	Open the Draw tab
ALT + Y + 3	Open the Help tab

In addition to these shortcuts, there are numerous shortcuts available to access specific commands within each tab.

Understanding the Workbook

In MS Excel, a Workbook consists of one or more Worksheets, also referred to as Sheets or spreadsheets. Each Worksheet is a separate tab within the Workbook and can contain different sets of data or information.

The structure and important components of a workbook are shown below.

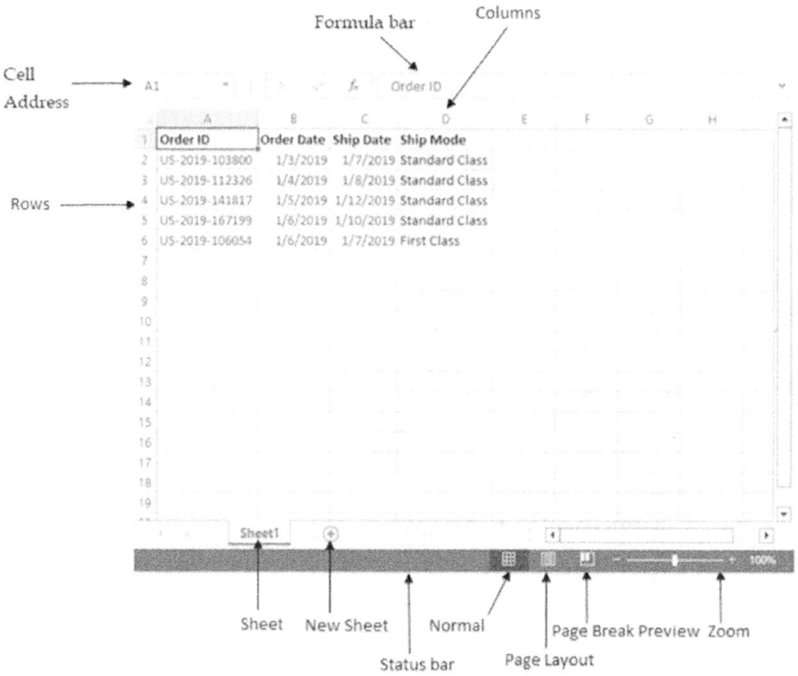

Figure 1.2: Workbook Structure.

Table 1.2 Workbook Structure explains the various components of a workbook.

Table:1.2 Workbook Structure.

Component	Description
Cell Address	Displays the active cell address which is an intersection of a row and a column. In this example, Order ID has the address A1.
Rows	Data in a spreadsheet is entered in rows and columns, with rows being numbered.
Columns	Columns are represented by alphabets.
Formula bar	Displays the data or formula in the active cell. Users can modify the contents of the cell or formula in this bar.
Sheet	When a new workbook is created, it displays one sheet by default. The name of the sheet can be changed.
New Sheet	The New sheet icon is used to add new sheets.
Status Bar	Depending on the data selected on the sheet, spreadsheets display the Count, Average, and Sum.
Normal	This option is used to view the spreadsheet in the normal mode.
Page Layout	This option is used to view the spreadsheet in a Page layout mode. It shows how the spreadsheet will appear when printed.
Page Break Preview	This option displays the Page Break preview.
Zoom	The slider can be used to zoom in or out.

Creating your first Workbook

Excel is all about entering data and formulas in the spreadsheet. Now that we have gained knowledge about the various components of Excel, let's create our first workbook.

Exercise1: Launch MS Excel and create an Excel workbook.
Enter data by referring to the enclosed data set in the *Practice* folder

Chapter1.MSExcelFundamentals.xlsx. It contains details of the orders made by the customers. The first row is the header, and the remaining rows contain data.

Refer Chapter1.MSExcelFundamentals_Solutions.xlsx in the Solutions folder for the solution.

Steps to create an Excel workbook:

1. Launch MS Excel. Click on the Windows button or press the Windows key on your keyboard, then type *Excel* and finally click on the *Excel* icon. This will open Microsoft Excel on your machine.
2. A screen will be displayed showing a *Blank workbook* along with various templates provided by MS Excel. Select *Blank workbook* to start with a new, empty workbook.

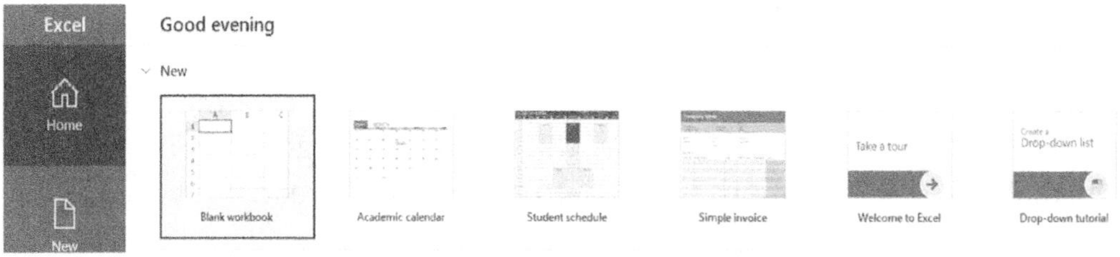

Figure 1.3: Select Blank workbook.

Selecting the *Blank workbook* icon will navigate to the spreadsheet development environment. It will display the ribbon on the top and an empty sheet called *Sheet1*.

3. Refer to the enclosed dataset Chapter1.MSExcelFundamentals.xlsx. Enter/type three rows of data in the empty spreadsheet. The first row is the header row, and the remaining two rows are for the data pertaining to the header.

	A	B	C	D	E	F	G	H	I	J	K	L	M
1	Row ID	Order ID	Order Date	Ship Mode	Ship Date	Customer ID	Segment	Region	Product ID	Sales	Quantity	Discount	Profit
2	1	US-2021-133949	1/1/2021	Priority Delivery	1/2/2021	JL-15175	Home Office	West	TEC-PH-908	475.944	7	0.2	59.493
3	2	US-2021-105249	2/1/2021	Standard Freight	2/10/2021	DH-13675	Home Office	West	FUR-BO-330	411.332	4	0.15	-4.8392

Figure 1.4: Three rows of data.

4. Each data element should be entered in a specific cell.
    a. Enter the data in a cell and press *Tab* key on the keyboard to navigate to the adjacent cell (horizontally).
    b. To go to the cell below (vertically), enter the data and press *Enter* on the keyboard.

The lines (dividing the column /letters) can be used to expand the cells.

Auto fill

Instead of manually typing data in each row/cell, use the AutoFill option to enter data more effortlessly.
AutoFill works on cells that follow a pattern, for example, the Row ID and Order Date columns. The Row ID column contains consecutive numbers (1, 2, 3, 4), and the Order Date column contains the first date of every month. However, AutoFill cannot be used on the Ship Date column, as it does not have any pattern.

Exercise2: Using the Auto fill feature, fill the remaining Row IDs 3 through 12. Also, use this option on Order Date to fill the continuous dates.

Steps to use the Auto fill feature:

1. In the worksheet, select the *Row ID* values 1 and 2, then use the fill handle (plus + sign) on the bottom right corner of the cell, and drag it down to fill the remaining Row IDs from 3 to 12.

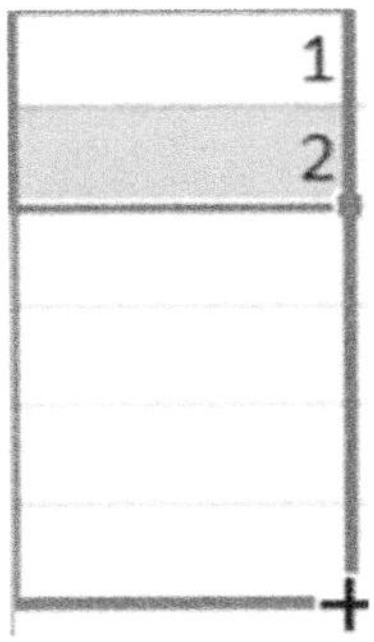

Figure 1.5: Auto fill on Row ID.

This will populate the remaining Row IDs in the rows below.

2. *Order Date* column follows a pattern, containing the first day of every month. We can also use Auto fill on this column. Select the first two dates on this column and drag them down to autofill the dates till 12/1/2021.

Figure 1.6: Auto fill on Order Date.

This will populate all the first days of every month.

Tip: To create consecutive dates using Autofill, select the first date value, and then drag the fill handle (plus + sign) down to auto fill the rest of the cells with consecutive dates.

The data in the other columns must be typed as they do not follow any pattern and therefore cannot be auto-filled. Enter the data in the remaining Columns by copying and pasting from Chapter1.MSExcelFundamentals.

Autofill is helpful in implementing formulas. A formula can be created for one cell and then filled in the remaining cells using Autofill.

Flash fill

Flash fill is a new feature in Excel 2023. It automatically fills the data in a column based on patterns it identifies in the adjacent cells. For example, Flash fill can be used to separate the first and second names from a single column or combine the first and second names from two different columns.

Exercise3: Using the Flash fill functionality, split *Ship Mode* into two separate columns.
Currently Ship Mode contains two words, for example, 'Priority Delivery'; the objective is to separate these values into two columns.
Refer to *Chapter1.MSExcelFundamentals_Solutions (Sheet EnteringData_FlashFill)* for the solution.

Steps to use the Flash fill:

1. In the worksheet created previously, insert two blank columns after the *Ship Mode* column. To do this, follow these steps:
   a. Highlight *Column E* by clicking on the column header. Right-click on the highlighted area and select *Insert*. This will insert one blank column after the *Ship Mode* column.
   b. Repeat the same step to insert another blank column, which will now be after the first blank column.
   This will result in two blank columns being inserted after the *Ship Mode* column.
2. After inserting the two blank columns after Ship Mode column, provide the headers of these new columns as Ship Name1 and Ship Name2.
3. In the *Ship Name 1* column, type the first name 'Priority' in the first cell. Then, use the right-click of the mouse and drag down from the edge of the cell to select *Flash Fill*. This will fill in the corresponding Ship Name1 values automatically based on the pattern it identifies.

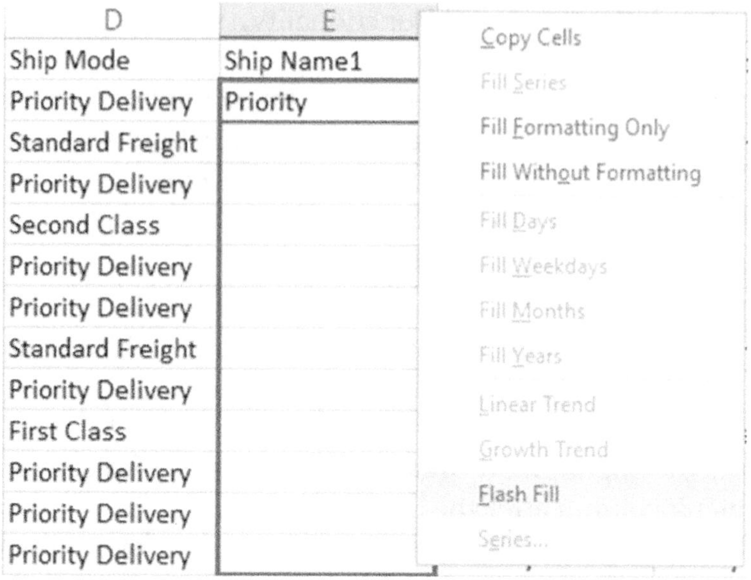

Figure 1.7: Flash Fill for Ship Name1.

4. Similarly, in the *Ship Name2* column, type the second name 'Delivery' in the first cell. Then, use the right-click of the mouse and drag down from the edge of the cell to select *Flash Fill*. This will fill in the corresponding *Ship Name2* values automatically based on the pattern it identifies.
5. To combine the columns again, insert a column after *Ship Name2*. Name this column header as *Ship Mode Combined*.
   In the first cell, type the combined name of the first Ship Mode – 'Priority Delivery'. Then, use the right-click of the mouse and drag down from the edge of the cell to select *Flash Fill*. This will fill in the corresponding combined Ship Modes automatically based on the pattern it identifies.

D	E	F	G
Ship Mode	Ship Name1	Ship Name2	Ship Mode Combined
Priority Delivery	Priority	Delivery	Priority Delivery
Standard Freight	Standard	Freight	Standard Freight
Priority Delivery	Priority	Delivery	Priority Delivery
Second Class	Second	Class	Second Class
Priority Delivery	Priority	Delivery	Priority Delivery
Priority Delivery	Priority	Delivery	Priority Delivery
Standard Freight	Standard	Freight	Standard Freight
Priority Delivery	Priority	Delivery	Priority Delivery
First Class	First	Class	First Class
Priority Delivery	Priority	Delivery	Priority Delivery
Priority Delivery	Priority	Delivery	Priority Delivery
Priority Delivery	Priority	Delivery	Priority Delivery

Figure 1.8: Flash fill output of Ship Mode.

Flash Fill can be used with any text values that follow a recognizable pattern. It automatically detects and fills the adjacent cells based on the identified pattern, making data manipulation and formatting more efficient.

Copy data from one sheet to another

The remaining data can be entered by referring to the enclosed Chapter1.MSExcelFundamentals.xlsx or copying the data from it.

Exercise4: Copy the data from Chapter1.MSExcelFundamentals.xlsx to a new sheet.

Steps to copy the data:

1. If the enclosed workbook is not already open, navigate to the enclosed data files and double click on Chapter1.MSExcelFundamentals_Solutions.xlsx.
2. Click on any cell and press *Ctrl* + *A* on the keyboard to select entire data on the sheet. Press *Ctrl* + *C* to copy the selected data.

3. Create a new sheet by clicking on the + sign next to the existing sheet name at the left bottom. Click on the first cell i.e. A1, and press *Ctrl + V* on the keyboard to paste the copied data.
4. Renaming the sheets.
   Right now, the new sheet will have the name as *Sheet2*. Rename the sheet by right-clicking on it and selecting *Rename*.

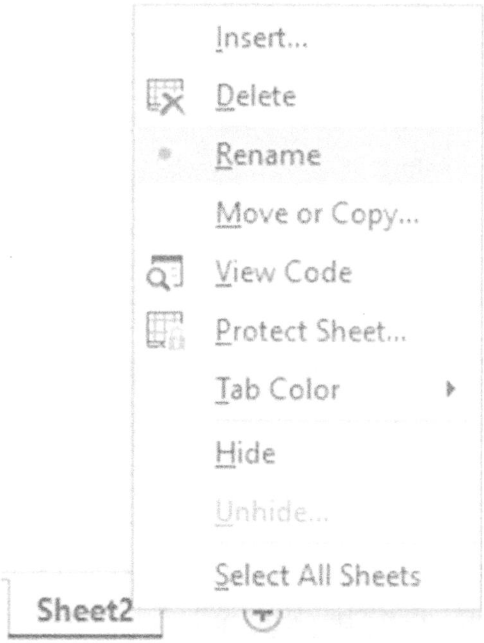

Figure 1.9: Renaming the sheet.

Rename the sheet as Copy_Original or any desired name.

The option *Move or Copy* as shown in Figure 1.9 is used to move or copy the spreadsheet within the existing Workbook. Try this option and observe the results.

Saving the Excel Workbook

To save the file for the first time, navigate to *File* option from the ribbon and select *Save As*. This option is used to save the file in the desired location. If the file is already saved, then use *Ctrl + S* keys on the keyboard to update the file in the existing location with the current changes made.

To save the workbook, navigate to *File* menu and select *Save As*. Then, select *Browse* to navigate to the desired location.

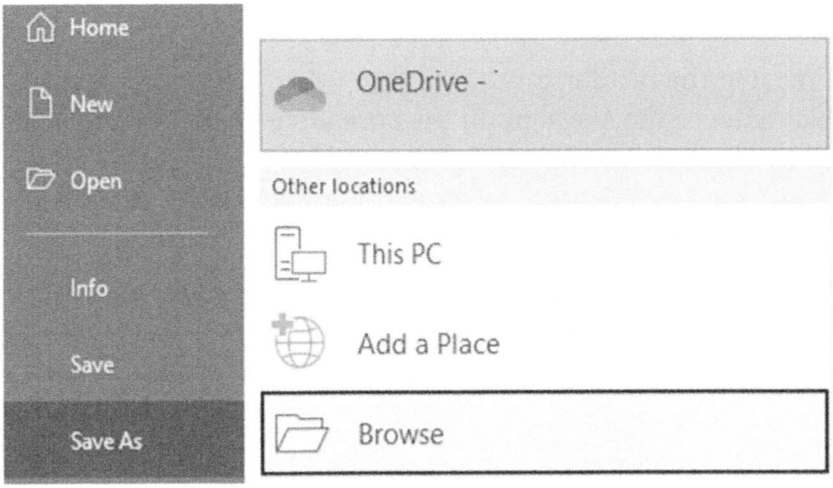

Figure 1.10: Browsing to a location.

After selecting the desired location, type the name of the file (to save the file with a different name) and choose *Save as type* as *Excel Workbook*.

Figure 1.11: File name and save as type.

As a best practice always save the file. The saved files will appear when the you open Excel next time.

Freeze Pane

The Freeze pane option keeps a specific area of the worksheet visible while scrolling vertically or horizontally. This option is available on the *View* tab of the ribbon, under the *Window* group.

Exercise5: Apply Freeze pane on the worksheet so that when user scrolls, the header row and the first column are always visible.
The current spread sheet contains 37 rows of data. If vertical scrolling is used, the header gets hidden, and if horizontal scrolling is used, the first column gets hidden. This can be fixed by using the Freeze feature.

Steps to Freeze the panes:

1. Freezing the header row.
   Navigate to the *View* tab in the spreadsheet ribbon and select *Freeze Panes,* then choose *Freeze Top Row.*

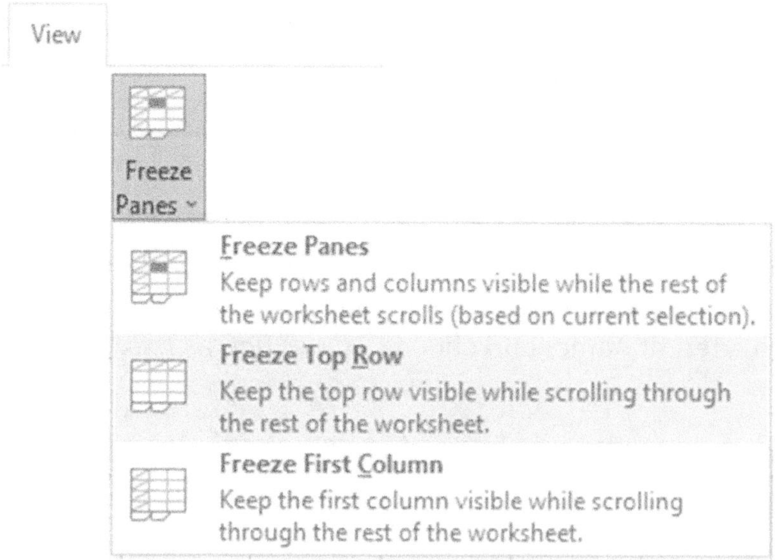

Figure 1.12: Freeze pane option.

A line will appear between the header row and the second row, indicating that the *Freeze Top Row* option has been implemented. Now, when scrolling down the sheet, the header row will remain visible.

2. Freeze first column.
   From *View/Freeze panes,* select *Freeze First Column.* When using horizontal scroll, the first column will always be visible.
3. Freeze multiple rows.
   Navigate to *View/Freeze panes* and select *Unfreeze pane* to reset the earlier option. Now, select the second row and first cell (A3). Navigate to *View/Freeze Panes* and select *Freeze Panes*. This will lock the first two rows from the top.
4. Freezing both Rows and Columns.
   Select a cell below the header row and to the right of the first column, i.e., cell B3. Navigate to *View/Freeze Panes* and select *Freeze Panes.* This will lock both the row and column together.

Freeze panes option is useful when the worksheet contains huge amounts of data.

Sorting

Sorting is the process of arranging a group of data in a specific order. In Excel, sorting can be performed on:

- Text fields (Alphabetical sorting), numbers (ascending or descending).
- Dates (oldest to newest and vice versa).
- Format (based on colors).
- Sorting can be performed on a single column or multiple columns.

Sorting options are available in the *Home* tab under *Editing* group or from the *Data* tab under *Sort & Filter* group (ALT + A + S).

Exercise6: In the previously saved workbook, sort the data first by Ship Mode in ascending order (A to Z), then by Segment in descending order (Z to A), and finally by Region in ascending order (A-Z).

Steps to perform Sorting using multiple columns:

1. Navigate to the *Data* tab in the ribbon and select *Sort*.

Figure 1.13: Sort option under Data tab.

2. A Sort dialog box will pop up with different options:
    - Sort By: Select *Ship Mode* from the dropdown to specify on which column the sorting will occur.
    - Sort On: Select *Cell Values* to specify how the sorting will be performed, i.e., on the cell Values or color.
    - Order: Select *A to Z* to specify the sort order i.e., ascending or descending. In this option, *Custom List* is used to specify the user-defined sorting pattern.

    Use *Add Level* to add other columns in the sorting, such as, *Segment* and *Region,* and select the appropriate settings.
    The Sort settings should appear as shown below:

Row ID	Order ID	Order Date	Ship Mode	Ship Name1	Ship Name2	Ship Mode Combined	Ship Date	Customer ID	Segment	Region	Product ID	Sales	Quantity	Discount	Profit
9	US-2021-120740	9/1/2021	First Class	First	Class	First Class	9/4/2021	PS-18970	Home Office	West	FUR-FU-333	187.76	4	0	76.981
19	US-2022-158680	7/1/2022	First Class	First	Class	First Class	7/4/2022	NZ-18565	Home Office	West	OFF-BI-768	2.496	1	0.2	0.904
23	US-2022-100671	11/1/2022	First Class	First	Class	First Class	11/4/2022	CS-12490	Corporate	Central	OFF-ST-769	111.67	9	0.2	6.979
26	US-2023-164147	2/1/2023	First Class	First	Class	First Class	2/4/2023	DW-13585	Corporate	East	OFF-FA-770	21.456	9	0.2	6.973
33	US-2023-169488	9/1/2023	First Class	First	Class	First Class	9/4/2023	AA-10375	Consumer	East	OFF-PA-773	39.96	2	0	18.781

Figure 1.14: Sorting on multiple columns.

This will rearrange the data in the Excel sheet according to the specified sorting criteria.

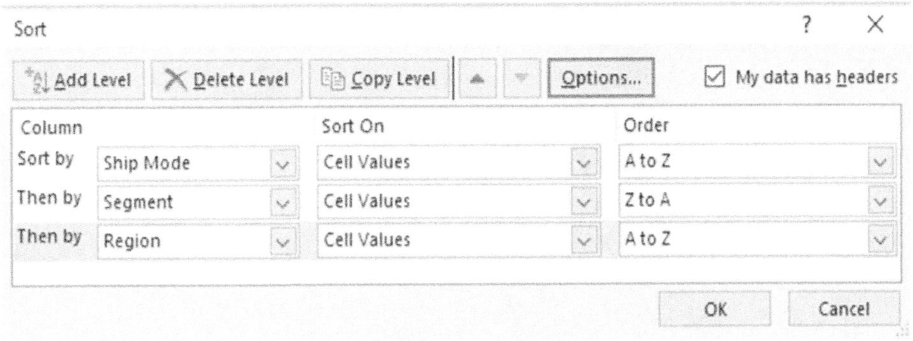

Figure 1.15: Display of data after sorting.

To reset the sorting, use the Undo command by pressing Ctrl + Z on the keyboard.

Filtering the data

Filters are used to display data based on specific criteria. Filters control what data is shown and what data is excluded.

Filters can be applied from either the *Home* tab under *Editing* group or the *Data* tab under *Sort & Filter* group.

They can be functional on both text and numeric columns, each offering different options. To display filtered data, use the selections from the list, search for specific values, or utilize comparison options in *Text* or *Number* filters.

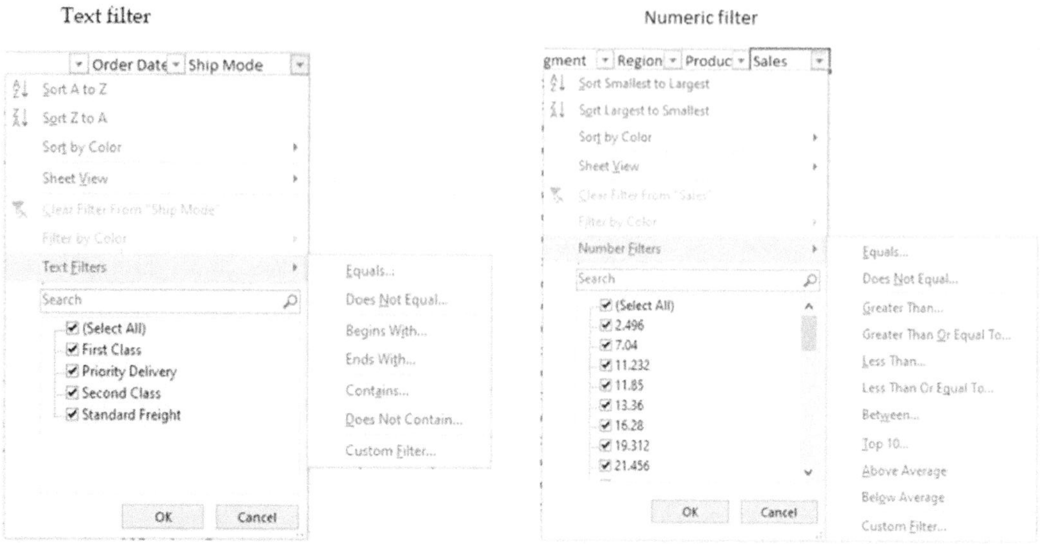

Figure 1.16: Text and Numeric filter options.

Exercise7: In the Excel file, Filter the data as follows:

- Filter by *Ship mode* as "First class" and then look for the data where *Sales* > 100.

Refer to Chapter1.MSExcelFundamentals_Solutions.xlsx (Filtered results sheet) in the Solutions folder *for the solution.*

Steps to apply Filters on the data:

1. Select any header column on the worksheet. Navigate to *Data* tab in the ribbon and select *Filter*. This will display drop-down arrows on each header column.
2. On the *Ship Mode* column, use the drop-down arrow. Uncheck *Select All* and select *First Class* from the list of Ship Mode values.

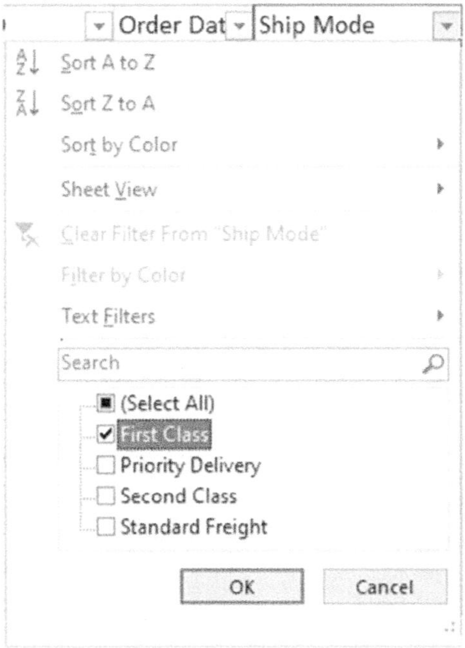

Figure 1.17: Filter on Ship Mode column.

This will filter the data by Ship Mode = First Class.

3. To apply filter for Sales > 100, perform the following two steps: From the Sales column drop-down, select Number Filters, then choose Greater Than. In the subsequent Custom Autofilter dialog, specify the condition as 100.

Figure 1.18: Filter on Sales Column.

This will display the *Sales* greater than 100 within *Ship Mode* First Class. The output will be as shown below:

Row ID	Order ID	Order Dat	Ship Mode	Ship Name	Ship Name	Ship Mode Combined	Ship Date	Customer I	Segment	Regio	Product ID	Sales	Quantit
9	US-2021-120740	9/1/2021	First Class	First	Class	First Class	9/4/2021	PS-18970	Home Offic	West	FUR-FU-333	187.76	4
17	US-2022-164784	5/1/2022	First Class	First	Class	First Class	5/4/2022	HF-14995	Consumer	South	FUR-FU-339	370.62	3
22	US-2022-157686	10/1/2022	First Class	First	Class	First Class	10/4/2022	BD-11620	Consumer	West	FUR-CH-342	194.848	4
23	US-2022-100671	11/1/2022	First Class	First	Class	First Class	11/4/2022	CS-12490	Corporate	Central	OFF-ST-769	111.672	9
29	US-2023-110198	5/1/2023	First Class	First	Class	First Class	5/4/2023	AG-10900	Consumer	South	FUR-BO-347	314.352	3
34	US-2023-129378	10/1/2023	First Class	First	Class	First Class	10/4/2023	NS-18505	Consumer	West	FUR-CH-348	108.608	4

Figure 1.19: Filtered data.

Task bar

The taskbar or status bar in an Excel spreadsheet is located at the bottom of the Excel window. It provides useful information and quick access to various functionalities. Taskbar displays the following:

- Ready status. The leftmost section typically displays "Ready" when Excel is idle and ready to receive user input.
- Sum, Average, Count. When range of cells containing numerical data is selected, Excel automatically shows the sum, average, and count of the selected cells on the bottom-right of the status bar.
- Zoom slider. The slider on the right end of the status bar allows users to adjust the zoom level of the worksheet.

- Page Layout and Normal View. Displayed on the right of the status bar. Clicking on these icons allows users to switch between these views for the worksheet.

Refer to Chapter1.MSExcelFundamentals_Solutions.xlsx, when Sales column is highlighted, MS Excel automatically displays Average, Count and Sum of the Sales.

Figure 1.20: Task bar results.

The taskbar (status bar) in Excel provides valuable information and quick access to frequently used features.

Printing in Excel

Printing data in an Excel worksheet allows users to produce hard copies of their spreadsheet for various purposes, such as reports, and presentations or data analysis. Entire or partial worksheet and workbooks can be printed. A Workbook can also be print to a file instead of a printer.

Printing Options

Several settings are available to print the data on an Excel worksheet. From the *File* menu in the ribbon, navigate to *Print* to view all the settings. The advantage of this option is that the user can see the preview of the data as they adjust the settings.
The shortcut to invoke the Print options is CTRL + P.

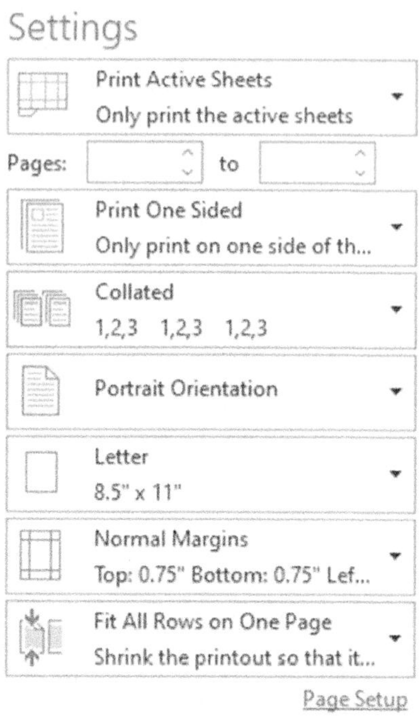

Figure 1.21: Print settings.

Table 1.3 Print settings explains the various options for printing Excel data.

Table:1.3 Printing options.

Printing Setting	**Description**
Print Active Sheets	Use this option to choose whether you want to print the entire workbook, the active sheet, or a selected area in the worksheet.
Print One sided	Use this option to specify whether you want to print only on one side of the paper or on both sides.
Collated	Refers to the way multiple copies of a document are arranged when printed. When you print multiple copies of a worksheet or workbook, the collate option determines whether the copies are printed sequentially or grouped together.
Portrait Orientation	Use this option to specify the orientation of the printed document - Portrait or Landscape.

Letter	This option is used to specify the size of the printed page.
Normal Margins	By looking at the preview of the data, you can adjust the margins of the document.
No scaling	The Scaling option can be used to specify how the data is to fit on a sheet while printing.
Page Setup	This option can be used to specify header and footer to the document while printing.

There are different print settings available to print data in an Excel worksheet. These options are also available from the ribbon's *Page Layout* tab.

Chapter 2

Formatting in Excel

The previous chapter provided an introduction to the fundamentals of MS Excel. This chapter will explore formatting in MS Excel, starting with basic cell formatting such as changing colors, fonts, and number formatting. In addition to the fundamental formatting options, the chapter will delve into conditional formatting, an advanced feature that enables automatic formatting based on specific conditions.

The following topics will be discussed in this chapter:

- Cell Formatting
- Conditional formatting

Cell Formatting in MS Excel

Formatting is used to provide meaning to the data stored in a cell and the overall sheet or workbook. For example, if a date is entered in a cell, it should appear as a date and not as a number. Formatting also involves coloring the cells, merging the cells, alignment, and conditional formatting.

The following types of formatting can be done in an Excel sheet:

- Providing background and text color to the data
- Changing the data format of the values
- Providing borders on the cells
- Suffixing numbers with $ and prefixing them with %
- Conditional formatting

To clear the applied formatting, navigate to *Home* tab and select *Clear* from the *Editing* group.

Format Cells

Format cells option can be applied to a specific cell or multiple cells in a worksheet. It is invoked by right-clicking on any cell and selecting *Format Cells* or by using the dialog box launcher (small downward arrow) on the *Number* group on the *Home* tab. The shortcut to invoke the Format Cell option is CTRL + 1.

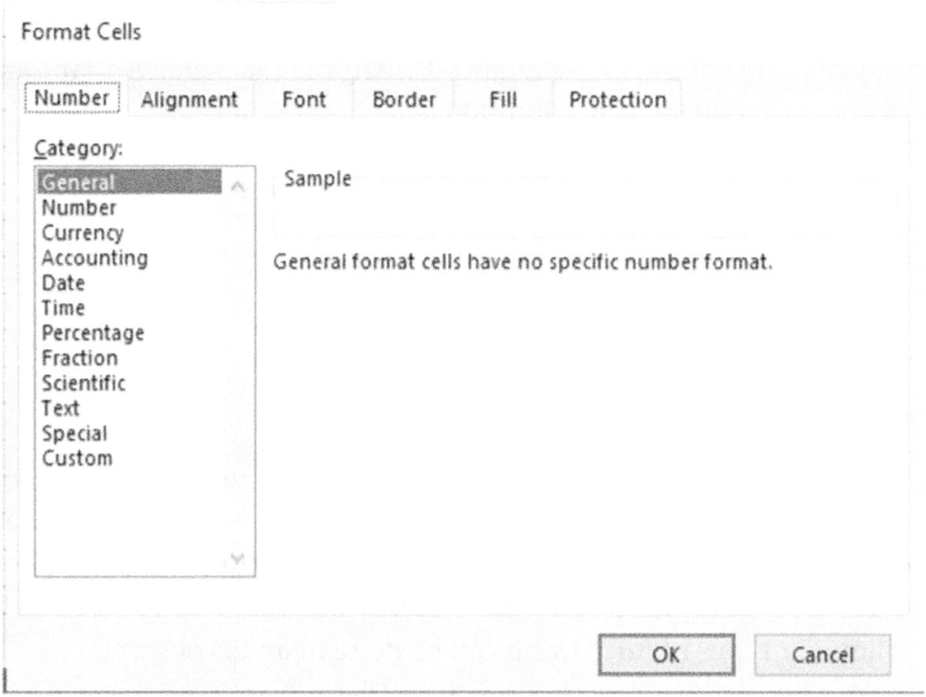

Figure 2.1: Format Cells options.

It consists of various tabs, including Number, Alignment, Font, Border, Fill, and Protection.

Table 2.1 lists the various options available on the *Format Cells* tabs.

Table:2.1 Format Cells tabs.

Tabs	Description
Number	Number option is used to specify what type of data is stored in a cell. It can be general or any of the number formats or a date.
Alignment	Used to provide Horizontal and Vertical alignment. It also has options for Wrap text, Shrink to fit, and Merge cells. Orientation of the text display can also be changed from here.
Font	Different Font styles can be specified from this tab.
Border	Borders around the cells can be controlled from this tab.
Fill	Fill is used to provide background colors to the cells.
Protection	This tab is used to protect the data in the cells, preventing others from making any changes. It works in conjunction with Review tab (Protect group) on the ribbon.

The tabs on Format Cells can also be accessed from the *Home* tab ribbon under the groups for *Font*, *Alignment*, and *Number*.

Exercise1: Use the enclosed Chapter2.FormattingInExcel.xlsx in the *Practice* folder.

Perform following formatting options.

- Make the Header row distinct by providing color and borders.
- Create a new row to group the header columns.
- Format the Sales, Discount, and Profit columns. Display Sales and Profit prefixed with a $ sign and two decimal places. Display Discount as a percentage.

Refer to Chapter2.FormattingInExcel_Solutions.xlsx (Cell Formatting sheet) in the Solutions folder for the solution.

Steps to format data in a worksheet:

1. Launch MS Excel and open Chapter2.FormattingInExcel.xlsx. Create a copy of the sheet or work on the same sheet.
2. Formatting headers.
   Headers should be distinct from the rest of the data. To do so, Highlight the header row (Row1, Columns A through M). From the *Home* tab, navigate to *Font* group and select *Fill Color*. Choose the desired color.

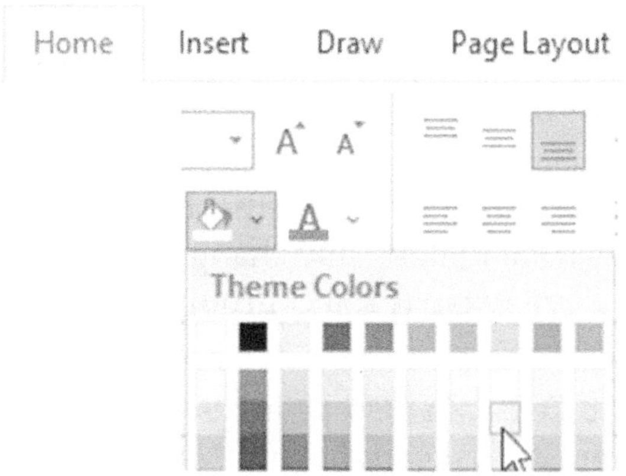

Figure 2.2: Background color for headers.

3. Select the header row again, and from the *Home* tab, under the *Font* group, select *Borders* and then *All borders*. This will produce borders around each cell in the header row.
4. Group the headers using merge cells.
   - Insert a blank row above the header row by selecting the header row, right-clicking, and selecting *Insert*.
   - In the new row, type *Order Details* in the cell with address B1 (first row, B column).
   - Select columns B1 through E1, and from the *Home* tab, select *Merge & Center* (from the *Alignment* group).

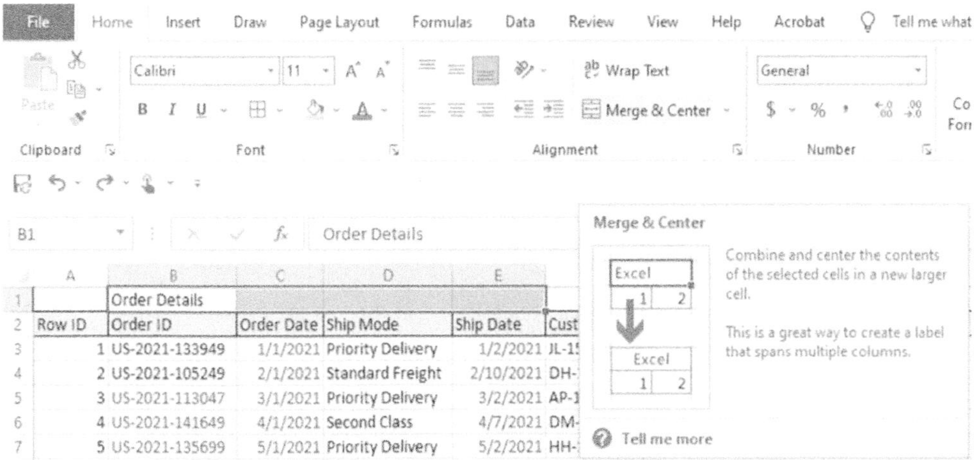

Figure 2.3: Merging cells.

This will display the text *Order Details* in the center of the selected cells.

To learn more details about the options used in MS-Excel to perform this formatting, select *Order Details*, right-click, and choose *Format Cells*.

- Similarly, type *Customer Details* in cell F1.
  Select cells F1 through I1 and from the *Home* tab, select *Merge & Center* (from *Alignment* group).
- Type *Metrics* in cell J1.
  Select cells J1 through M1 and from the *Home* tab, select *Merge & Center* (from Alignment group).
- Use different colors to differentiate the groups.

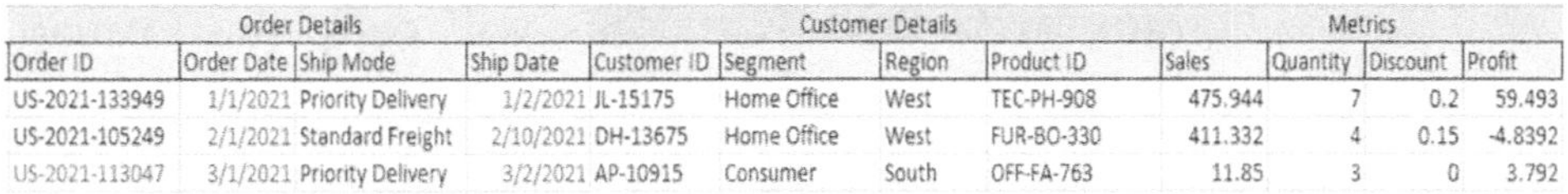

Order Details				Customer Details				Metrics			
Order ID	Order Date	Ship Mode	Ship Date	Customer ID	Segment	Region	Product ID	Sales	Quantity	Discount	Profit
US-2021-133949	1/1/2021	Priority Delivery	1/2/2021	JL-15175	Home Office	West	TEC-PH-908	475.944	7	0.2	59.493
US-2021-105249	2/1/2021	Standard Freight	2/10/2021	DH-13675	Home Office	West	FUR-BO-330	411.332	4	0.15	-4.8392
US-2021-113047	3/1/2021	Priority Delivery	3/2/2021	AP-10915	Consumer	South	OFF-FA-763	11.85	3	0	3.792

Figure 2.4: Grouped cells in different colors.

5. Number formatting.
   To format Sales values to display the $ sign.
   - Select the Sales column (Column J).

- Go to the *Home* tab and navigate to the *Number* group
- Click on the drop-down arrow next to the Number Format box.
- Select *Accounting* from the list of number formats.
  Now the Sales will be displayed with the $ sign and two decimal places.

Figure 2.5: Changing the format of a number.

If some of the cells display hash (#), that means that value is too large to fit in the cell. To view the complete value, use the mouse to drag the column boundary to extend the column width.

Tip: Number formats can also be changed by right-clicking on the selected cells and choosing *Format Cells.*

6. Utilizing format painter.
   The *Profit* column should also have the same format as *Sales*. To do this, follow these steps:
   - Select any cell in *Column J* (*Sales*)
   - Go to the *Home* tab, find *Format Painter* icon in the *Clipboard* group, and click on it. This will copy the formatting of the selected cell.

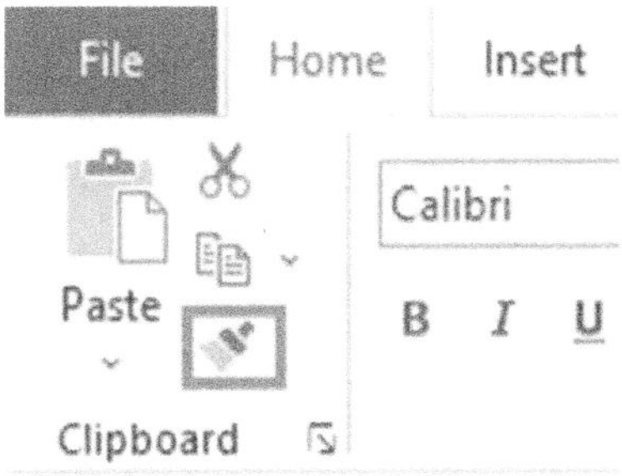

Figure 2.6: Selecting Format painter.

- Now select or drag over all the values in *Column M* (Profit). This will apply the format of the Sales column to the Profit column.

Tip: If user click on the Format Painter once, it will copy the formatting, which can only be pasted once. To paste the formatting at multiple locations, click on the Format Painter, then click on the desired locations. If user double-click on the Format Painter icon, the formatting can be pasted at multiple locations with clicking again. To reset the copied formatting at any time, press the *Esc* key on the keyboard.

7. Formatting Discount column to display as a percentage (%).
   Select *Column L (Discount)* and from the *Home* tab, navigate to the *Number* group, then click on the % icon to format the values as percentages.

Formatting of data is essential to ensure that the data entered is displayed in the intended format. To review or change the format, right-click on the cell and select *Format Cells.*

Conditional Formatting

Conditional formatting in Excel allows users to apply formatting to the data based on specific criteria. It is similar to Cell formatting but more dynamic as it is based on conditions. Conditional formatting options are available from the *Home* tab under *Styles,* in the Conditional Formatting group.

Figure 2.7: Conditional Formatting options.

The shortcut to invoke the Conditional Formatting options is ALT + H + L.

MS Excel provides predefined conditional formatting options such as Highlight Cells Rules, Top/Bottom Rules, etc. Custom rules can be defined by using the *New Rule* option. To reset the formatting options, select *Clear Rules*.

Exercise2: Perform the following formatting options in the worksheet data.

- Display the Sales amount in Green where Sales is greater than $500.
- Display negative Profits in red.
- Display Top 20% of Profit in green.
- Display data bars to represent higher and lower quantities sold.
- Display Sales Score card to depict Low, Medium, and High sales amounts in red, yellow, and green, respectively.

Refer to *Chapter2. FormattingInExcel_Solutions (Conditional Formatting sheet) for the solution.*

Steps to perform Conditional formatting:

1. Use the previously saved sheet. Either make a copy of it or work on the same sheet.
2. Display Sales in Green.
   - Select Column J (Sales). From the ribbon, navigate to *Home> Styles > Conditional Formatting.*
   - From *Conditional Formatting,* select the option for *Greater Than.* In the *Greater Than* dialog, specify the condition for greater than 500 and choose the color *Green fill with Dark Green Text.*

     Steps shown as 1 and 2 in the figure below.

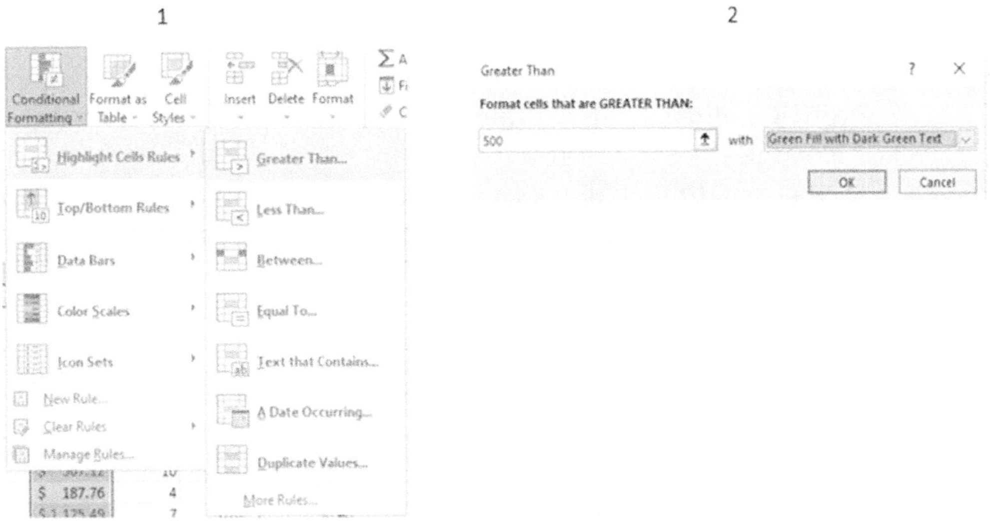

Figure 2.8: Sales greater than $500.

This will display *Sales* greater than $500 in green color.

3. Display negative *Profits* in red.
   - Select Column M (Profit). From the ribbon, navigate to *Home> Styles > Conditional Formatting.*

- From *Conditional Formatting*, select the option for *Highlight Cells Rules* and then choose *Less Than* and in the *Less Than* dialog box, specify the condition for negative values.

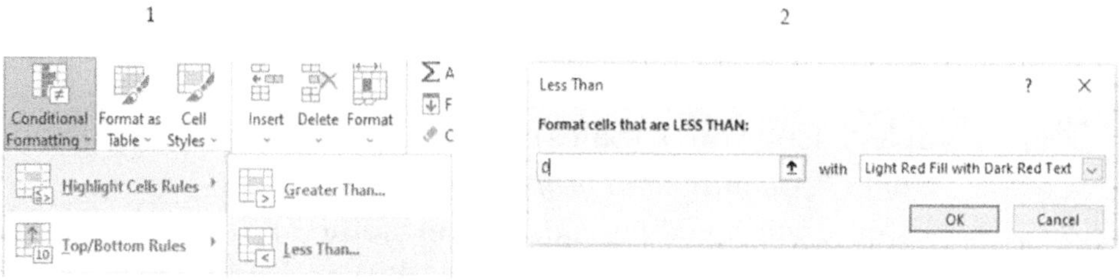

Figure 2.9: Display negative Profits in red.

This will display negative Profits in red.

4. Display Top 20% of Profit in Green.
   - Select Column M (Profit). From the ribbon, navigate to *Home> Styles > Conditional Formatting.*
   - From *Conditional Formatting,* choose the option for *Top/Bottom Rules* and choose *Top 10%.*
   - In the *Top 10%* dialog box, specify the condition for 20% and change the color to *Green fill with Dark Green Text.*

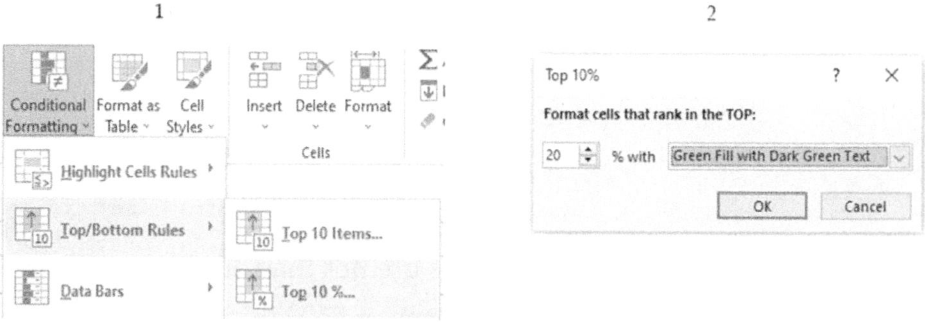

Figure 2.10: Displaying Top 20% of Profit.

This will display the Top 20% of Profit amounts in Green.

5. Display data bars on Quantity.
   - Select Column K (Quantity). From the ribbon, navigate to *Home > Styles > Conditional Formatting.*

- From *Conditional Formatting*, choose the option for *Data Bars* and select the desired bar colors.

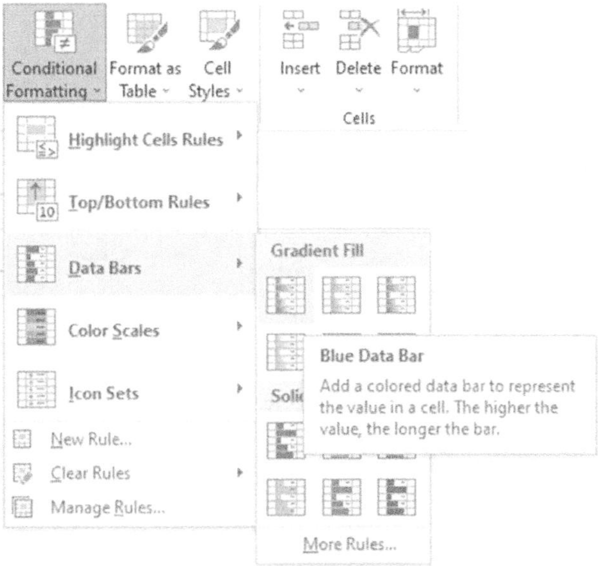

Figure 2.11: Displaying data bars on Quantity.

The length of the bar will represent higher and lower quantities.

6. Display Sales score card.
   For this example, copy the *Sales* column into an empty column after *Profit* and name it as *New Sales*. This is done so that the previous formatting is not disturbed.
   - Select *New Sales* column and from *Conditional Formatting*, choose *Clear Rules* and then select *Clear Rules from Selected Cells*. This will remove all the previous formatting.
   - With the New Sales column selected, from *Conditional Formatting*, choose the option for *Color Scales* and select the first color scale.

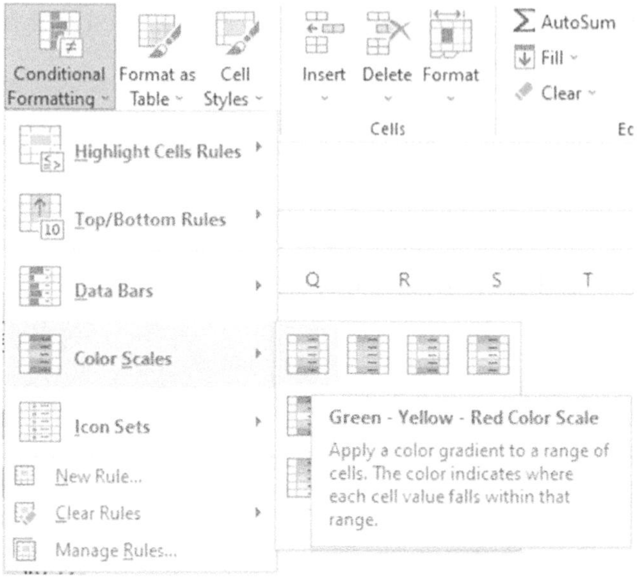

Figure 2.12: Use color scales to display the Scorecard.

This will display high Sales in Green, medium in Yellow, and lower Sales in red.

Custom Conditional Formatting

Custom conditional formatting allows users to define custom formatting rules instead of using the Excel predefined rules (explained in the previous section.) Custom formatting rules are defined from Home > Styles > Conditional Formatting > New Rule.

Exercise3: Use the previous worksheet for this exercise.

- Color the *Segment* in Yellow color where Sales > 500.

For solution, refer to *Chapter2.FormattingInExcel_Solutions (Conditional Formatting sheet)*.

Steps to perform Custom conditional formatting:

1. Select the data portion of Column G (Segment), i.e., G3 to G38. Navigate to the *Home* tab and then click on *Conditional Formatting > New Rules.*
2. Under the *New Formatting Rules* box, select the last option *Use Formula to determine which cells to format.*
3. Under *Edit Rule description*, type the formula,

```
=$J3 > 500
```

Where J3 is the address of the Sales column (starting cell).

Note: In the above calculation, the $ sign is prefixed to provide absolute referencing. It will keep the J column absolute and unchanged when the calculation occurs for each row.

4. Click on *Format* at the bottom of the screen and in the subsequent *Format Cells* dialog box, go to the *Fill* tab, and select Yellow color.

   The above steps are shown in the figure below as Step1, Step 2, and Step 3.

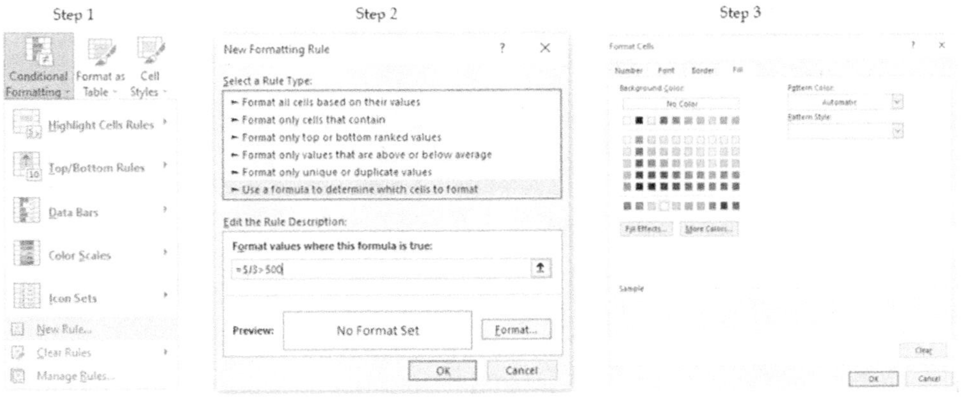

Figure 2.13: Highlighting Segment where Sales is greater than 500.

This will highlight Segment cells in yellow where Sales > 500.

To edit the rules, navigate to *Conditional Formatting > Manage Rules.*
To clear the applied formatting anytime, navigate to *Conditional Formatting > Clear Rules.*

Using conditional formatting, based on a condition different types of formatting options can be applied.

Excel's formatting capabilities are essential for creating visually appealing and informative spreadsheets.
With this knowledge, users can confidently format their data, making it more impactful and insightful for their audience. Understanding the various formatting options available in Excel empowers users to present their data effectively and efficiently.

Chapter 3
Introduction to Formulas

The previous chapter explained various formatting options in Excel. This chapter will delve into Formulas, one of the most powerful features in Excel. Additionally, we will explore different types of Cell references in Excel, as they are essential for understanding formulas.

The following topics will be discussed in this chapter:

- Overview of Formulas
- Cell reference
- Copy values of a formula

Overview of Formulas

A formula in Excel is a mathematical expression that performs calculations or actions on the data present in the worksheet.

- A formula can be written in any cell and always starts with an equal (=) sign followed by an expression. After typing the formula, press the Enter key on the keyboard to execute it.
- A formula can contain a mathematical operator (+, -, /, *) or an Excel-defined function (Sum, Average, Min, Max, etc.).
- If functions are used in a formula, they are always enclosed within a pair of parentheses ( ).
- A formula in a cell can be used with autofill to compute the formula for all the rows and columns.
- To execute/finalize a formula, press *Enter* on the keyboard. To exit from the formula cell. press the *ESC* key on the keyboard.
- A formula can contain a cell address, a range of cells (vertical or horizontal), a function, a mathematical operator, or a constant.

For example, the following formula:

```
=SUM(C3:C14) * 2
```

uses Sum function to add the values contained in the cell range C3 through C14 and finally multiplies it by a constant 2. A constant is a number or text values entered directly into a formula, and these values do not change.

- When a Formula is typed, it appears in the formula Bar at the top of the sheet. To view a formula, select a cell containing the formula, and it will be displayed in the formula bar.

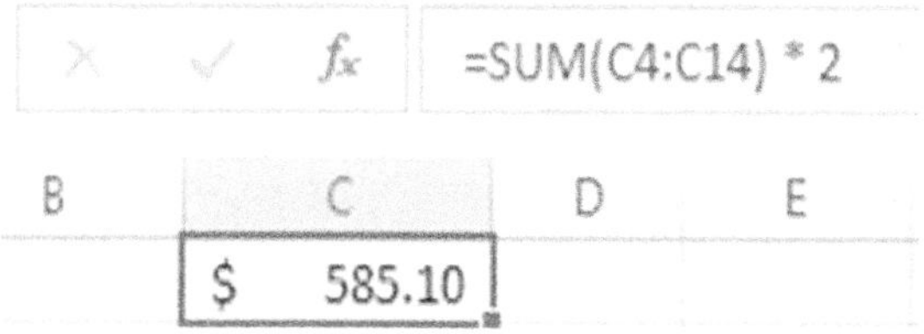

Figure 3.1: Formula bar.

A formula can be copied and pasted between the cells, and it can refer to cells in the same worksheet, different worksheets in the same workbook, or even worksheets in different workbooks.

- All available functions in Excel can be accessed by clicking on *fx* in the formula bar.
  The shortcut to invoke the Formula tab is ALT + M.

Tip: Formulas usually refer to a range of cells. To select all the cells in a column, click on the first cell and then press CTRL+ SHIFT and the down arrow on the keyboard.

Exercise1: Use the enclosed Chapter3.IntrotoFormula.xlsx (Original Sheet) to perform this exercise.
The workbook contains the payroll data for employees, including their Last name, First name, Hourly Wage, and Hours worked. There is a blank column for Pay as of June 9th. Perform the following calculations:

- Calculate the Pay for June 9th for each employee
- Calculate the Totals, Maximum, Minimum, and Average values for the Hourly Wage and June 9 Pay columns.

Refer to Chapter3. IntrotoFormula_Solutions.xlsx (BasicFormulas sheet) for the solution.

Steps to perform calculations:

1. Open the file Chapter3.IntrotoFormula.xlsx and review the data.
2. Calculate Pay for June 9th.
   - Click on cell F3, type "=", and then click on cell C3 (Hourly Wage of the first employee).
   - Type "*", and then click on cell D3 (Hours worked for the first employee) and press enter.
     This will calculate the Pay of the first employee with a formula

     ```
     =C3*D3
     ```

   - Using the mouse, Autofill (click on the cell and drag it down from the edge) the rest of the cells to perform the calculation for rest of the rows.
3. Calculate the Total Hourly Wage.
   - Navigate to cell B15 and type the Text *Total.*
   - On cell C15, type "=", and then type the function, *Sum*. Since it is a function, it should be enclosed in parenthesis, type "(". We can press *Tab* on the keyboard after typing =Sum.
   - Using the mouse, select the range on Column C (Hourly Wage).
   - Close the parenthesis and press *Enter*.

Hourly Wage	
$	45.90
$	32.50
$	20.00
$	25.70
$	30.60
$	50.00
$	10.50
$	16.75
$	18.30
$	27.60
$	14.70

=Sum(C3:C13)

Figure 3.2: Calculating the Sum.

4. Calculate Maximum Hourly Wage.
   - In cell B16 type the Text *Max.*
   - In cell C16, type "=Max(" (or press Tab on your keyboard after typing =Max).
   - Using the mouse, select the range in Column C (Hourly Wage).
   - Close the parenthesis and press Enter. The maximum hourly wage will be displayed in cell C16, and the formula should look like the following:

```
=MAX(C3:C13)
```

5. Calculate Minimum Hourly Wage.
   - Navigate to cell B17 and type the Text *Min.*
   - On cell C17, type "=Min(" or press Tab on your keyboard after typing =Min.
   - Using the mouse, select the range on Column C (Hourly Wage).
   - Close the parenthesis and press enter. The minimum hourly wage will be displayed in cell C17, the formula should look like the following:

```
=Min(C3:C13)
```

6. Calculate Average Hourly Wage.
   - Go to cell B18 and type the Text *Average.*
   - Select cell C18 and type "=Average(".
   - Using the mouse, select the range on Column C (Hourly Wage).
   - Close the parenthesis and press Enter. The average hourly wage will be displayed in cell C18 and the formula should look like the following:

```
=Average(C3:C13)
```

7. Calculate Total, Max, Min and Average for the Pay column.
   - Copy the formulas performed previously in columns C15, C16, C17, and C18.
   - Select cell F15 and paste the copied formulas in F15. Excel will automatically adjust the cell references for F15, F16, F17, and F18 to reflect the appropriate values from the Pay column.

After performing the above calculations, the worksheet will look like the one shown below:

Last Name	First Name	Hourly Wage	Hours Worked	Shift	9-Jun
Smith	Adam	$ 45.90	41	Day	$ 1,881.90
Shin	Mark	$ 32.50	42	Day	$ 1,365.00
Keller	Shawn	$ 20.00	49	Night	$ 980.00
Hay	Kayal	$ 25.70	41	Day	$ 1,053.70
Sharma	Rekha	$ 30.60	39	Day	$ 1,193.40
Costanza	David	$ 50.00	44	Day	$ 2,200.00
Schultz	Patrick	$ 10.50	55	Night	$ 577.50
Jonas	Nick	$ 16.75	33	Night	$ 552.75
Gill	Suraj	$ 18.30	29	Night	$ 530.70
Reynolds	Mike	$ 27.60	40	Day	$ 1,104.00
Lenge	John	$ 14.70	30	Night	$ 441.00
	Total	$ 292.55			$ 11,879.95
	Max	$ 50.00			$ 2,200.00
	Min	$ 10.50			$ 441.00
	Average	$ 26.60			$ 1,080.00

Figure 3.3: Worksheet with Calculations.

Cell Reference

When creating a formula or calculation in Excel, it refers to the data in a cell or a range of cells. This reference can be made to cells in any part of the same worksheet, different worksheets in the same workbook, or even in other workbooks. As seen in the previous exercise, a range of cells is denoted by a colon, i.e., C3:C13 represents the range of cells from C3 through C13.

In a formula, a reference to a cell is made in five ways -

- Relative cell reference
- Absolute cell reference
- Mixed cell reference
- 3-D cell reference
- R1C1 cell reference

Relative Cell reference

Relative cell reference in Excel allows formulas to calculate based on their position relative to the cells they refer to. This makes it easier to copy and apply formulas across different cells, rows, and columns.

- Relative cell reference is based on the relative position of the cell containing the formula and the cell/data it refers to.
- If the position of the cell containing the formula changes, its reference also changes accordingly.
- If the formula is copied to other rows or columns, the reference automatically adjusts to reflect the new location.
- By default, all formulas use relative references.

Refer to previous exercise Step 4. Pay was calculated using the formula =C3*D3 in cell F3. When the formula is auto filled in the remaining columns, Excel automatically changed the reference to the respective cells.

```
=C3*D3
=C4*D4
=C5*D5
=C6*D6
=C7*D7
=C8*D8
=C9*D9
=C10*D10
=C11*D11
=C12*D12
=C13*D13
```

Figure 3.4: Relative Reference.

Click on each cell to check the formula. When the Total, Max, Min, and Average calculations were copied and pasted (previous exercise Step 7), relative referencing was used again.

Tip: To display the formula used in the entire sheet, use the *Show Formula* toggle located in *Formulas > Formula Auditing* on the ribbon. This will switch between the actual formula and the resulting value.

Absolute Cell reference

Absolute cell references always point to a specific cell address. If the position of the cell containing the formula changes, the absolute reference remains constant. Unlike relative references, if a formula with absolute references is copied or auto-filled, the references do not change.

To create an absolute reference, use a $ sign before the respective column and row. For example, to make an absolute reference to cell G1, the syntax will be $G$1.

Exercise2: Use the enclosed Chapter3. IntrotoFormula.xlsx (Absolute Reference Sheet) to perform this exercise.

- Calculate Nightly incentive.
  If the *Shift* (Column E) is 'Night', multiply the Hourly wage with the % value provided in cell G1 for the Shift Incentive.

- Calculate Total Pay by adding the values of the Nightly incentive column to Pay (Column F).

Refer to Chapter3_IntrotoFormula_Solutions.xlsx (Absolute Reference sheet) for the solution.

Since this exercise involves using a condition, we will first understand the IF Function.

IF Function

An IF function evaluates a logical expression and displays a value if it is true, and another value if it is false.

Syntax:

=IF (logical_test, value_if_True, value_if_false)

Steps to perform Absolute Cell Reference calculation:

1. Open Chapter3.IntrotoFormula.xlsx (Absolute reference sheet) and navigate to *Nightly Incentive* (Column G).
2. In cell G4, type the IF condition to check the value of the *Shift* (Column E).
   If Shift = Night, multiply the corresponding Hourly wage with the % value available in the cell G1; otherwise show 0.

   ```
   =IF(E4="Night", C4*G1,0)
   ```

   Press *Enter* on the keyboard after typing the formula.

   Tip: To avoid typing the cell references for E4, C4, and G1, click on those cells and they will be automatically included in the formula.

   The result of the calculation in column G4 will be 0 as the corresponding *Shift* for this column is Day.
3. Use Auto fill (click on G4, use the + icon on the edge and drag it down) to fill the rest of the cells in column G.

Nightly Incentive
0
0
#VALUE!
0
0
0
0
0
0
0
0
0
0
0
0
0

Figure 3.5: Incorrect result of the formula.

Notice that the values are incorrect, and an error is displayed in one cell.

What is the reason for the incorrect results?

The calculation is supposed to multiply each cell with G1 (% value) when Shift = "Night"; therefore, the first calculation is correct (on Cell G4). However, when autofill was performed, Excel used relative reference and changed G1 to G2, G3, G4, etc.

To resolve this error, the calculation needs to be modified to include the absolute reference for G1 so that it does not change.

4. To fix the incorrect results, delete all the data in column G (for the formula) and modify the calculation in G4 as

```
=IF(E4 = "Night",C4*$G$1,0)
```

Then perform autofill. Now the correct values will be displayed.

Nightly Incentive
0
0
3
0
0
0
1.575
2.5125
2.745
0
2.205
0
0
0
0
0

Figure 3.6: Correct results with Absolute referencing.

Absolute referencing is employed when the cell address in the formula needs to remain the constant or fixed. This ensures that the formula does not change when it is copied or filled to other cells.

5. Calculate Total Pay.
   - In the column next to Nightly Incentive (Column H), add the text for the header as '9-Jun Total Pay'.
   - Add the calculation to sum the values in Column F and Column G.

```
=F4+G4
```

   Autofill all the cells in column H.

6. Copy the totals from Column F (F16 through F19) and paste them on Column H starting from H16. The values will automatically adjust accordingly.

The final output will appear as below:

					Shift Incentive Pay	15%	
Last Name	First Name	Hourly Wage	Hours Worked	Shift	9-Jun	Nightly Incentive	9-Jun Total Pay
Smith	Adam	$ 45.90	41	Day	$ 1,881.90	0	$ 1,881.90
Shin	Mark	$ 32.50	42	Day	$ 1,365.00	0	$ 1,365.00
Keller	Shawn	$ 20.00	49	Night	$ 980.00	3	$ 983.00
Hay	Kayal	$ 25.70	41	Day	$ 1,053.70	0	$ 1,053.70
Sharma	Rekha	$ 30.60	39	Day	$ 1,193.40	0	$ 1,193.40
Costanza	David	$ 50.00	44	Day	$ 2,200.00	0	$ 2,200.00
Schultz	Patrick	$ 10.50	55	Night	$ 577.50	1.575	$ 579.08
Jonas	Nick	$ 16.75	33	Night	$ 552.75	2.5125	$ 555.26
Gill	Suraj	$ 18.30	29	Night	$ 530.70	2.745	$ 533.45
Reynolds	Mike	$ 27.60	40	Day	$ 1,104.00	0	$ 1,104.00
Lenge	John	$ 14.70	30	Night	$ 441.00	2.205	$ 443.21
	Total	$ 292.55			$ 11,879.95		$ 11,891.99
	Max	$ 50.00			$ 2,200.00		$ 2,200.00
	Min	$ 10.50			$ 441.00		$ 443.21
	Average	$ 26.60			$ 1,080.00		$ 1,081.09

Figure 3.7: Final output with Absolute reference.

Mixed Cell reference

Mixed Cell Reference combines both relative and absolute cell references. It can have either of the two flavors:

- Absolute row (for e.g., G$1) and Relative column. If copied or auto filled, the row remains unchanged while the column changes.
- Absolute column (for e.g., $G1) and Relative row. If copied or auto filled, the column remains unchanged and the row changes.

Exercise3: Use the provided Chapter3.IntrotoFormula.xlsx (Sheet Mixed Reference_1) to perform this exercise.
This sheet contains Gross pay of the employees for different Weeks and their deductions.

- For each month, calculate Net Pay as Gross Pay – (Gross * Deduction)

This exercise will use Mixed reference type 1 where column is absolute, and the row is relative.

Refer to Chapter3. IntrotoFormula_Solutions.xlsx (Mixed Reference sheet_1) for the solution.

Steps to perform Mixed cell reference calculation:

1. On Chapter3.*IntrotoFormula_*.xlsx (Sheet Mixed reference_1), navigate to titled *9-Jun Net Pay* (Column G).
2. On Cell G3, type the calculation for *Net Pay* as follows:

```
=C3 - (C3*F3)
```

   After typing the formula, press Enter. Then, use the autofill handle to fill the formula in the rest of the cells in Column G. All the values will be calculated correctly. This can be checked by selecting each of the cells to verify the calculations.
3. Now to get the values for the week starting 23-Jun, perform Autofill horizontally.

9-Jun	23-Jun
Net Pay	Net Pay
$ 1,787.81	
$ 1,296.75	
$ 963.34	
$ 1,022.09	
$ 1,157.60	
$ 2,112.00	
$ 573.28	
$ 549.71	
$ 528.11	
$ 1,081.92	
$ 438.77	

Figure 3.8: Horizontal Autofill.

This will produce incorrect results.

What is the reason for the incorrect results?

On cell H3, the current displayed calculation is =D3 - (D3*G3). While D3 is correct, the *Deduction* column reference is shown as G3 instead of F3. This is due to Excel's default use of relative referencing, which changed F3 to G3 when the formula was copied to the new column using horizontal autofill.

The objective is to keep the *Deduction* column (F) constant but change the rows (values vertically). To achieve this, the calculation in G3 needs to be modified to include the Mixed reference for Column F (F$3) so that the column does not change when autofill is used.

4. To fix the incorrect results, delete all the data in column G (for the formula) and modify the calculation in G4 as:

```
=C3 - (C3*$F3)
```

Tip: To add a $ sign for mixed reference, first type the regular calculation, and then in the formula bar, add $ before the respective column or row.

Now, perform autofill both vertically and horizontally for all the weeks. The correct values will be displayed. The usage of $F3 in the formula will keep the column F constant and change only the rows, allowing the calculations to be correctly applied.

The final output will appear as shown below:

		9-Jun	23-Jun	7-Jul		9-Jun	23-Jun	7-Jul
Last Name	First Name	Gross Pay	Gross Pay	Gross Pay	Deductions	Net Pay	Net Pay	Net Pay
Smith	Adam	$1,881.90	$1,836.00	$ 1,790.10	5%	$ 1,787.81	$ 1,744.20	$ 1,700.60
Shin	Mark	$1,365.00	$1,462.50	$ 1,560.00	5%	$ 1,296.75	$ 1,389.38	$ 1,482.00
Keller	Shawn	$ 983.00	$ 760.00	$ 537.00	2%	$ 963.34	$ 744.80	$ 526.26
Hay	Kayal	$1,053.70	$1,336.40	$ 1,619.10	3%	$ 1,022.09	$ 1,296.31	$ 1,570.53
Sharma	Rekha	$1,193.40	$1,009.80	$ 826.20	3%	$ 1,157.60	$ 979.51	$ 801.41
Costanza	David	$2,200.00	$1,500.00	$ 800.00	4%	$ 2,112.00	$ 1,440.00	$ 768.00
Schultz	Patrick	$ 579.08	$ 336.00	$ 92.93	1%	$ 573.28	$ 332.64	$ 92.00
Jonas	Nick	$ 555.26	$ 753.75	$ 952.24	1%	$ 549.71	$ 746.21	$ 942.72
Gill	Suraj	$ 533.45	$ 786.90	$ 1,040.36	1%	$ 528.11	$ 779.03	$ 1,029.95
Reynolds	Mike	$1,104.00	$ 883.20	$ 662.40	2%	$ 1,081.92	$ 865.54	$ 649.15
Lenge	John	$ 443.21	$ 588.00	$ 732.80	1%	$ 438.77	$ 582.12	$ 725.47

Figure 3.9: Final output with Absolute column Mixed reference.

Exercise4: Use the enclosed Chapter3.*IntrotoFormula*.xlsx (Sheet Mixed Reference_2) to perform this exercise.
This sheet contains the Salary of the employees and % spent on various Expenses such as Grocery, Rent, and Movies.

- Calculate Actual amounts spent by employees on each of these expenses by multiplying the Pay with each of the expenses % values.

This exercise will use both types of Mixed references - Row absolute/Column relative and Column absolute/Row relative.

Refer to Chapter3.IntrotoFormula_Solutions.xlsx (Sheet Mixed Reference sheet_2) for the solution.

Steps to perform Mixed cell reference for both the types of calculations:

1. Open Chapter3.*IntrotoFormula*.xlsx (Sheet Mixed reference_2).
2. For Grocery.
    - Navigate to *Grocery Amount* (Cell D6).
    - Create a calculation by typing "=" and then select the cell for Pay (C6), then type "*" and then select the cell for Grocery % (C2). The calculation should look like:

```
=C6*C2
```

3. Autofill the values horizontally to get values for *Rent Amount* and *Movie Amount* for the first employee Adam Smith, and observe the results.

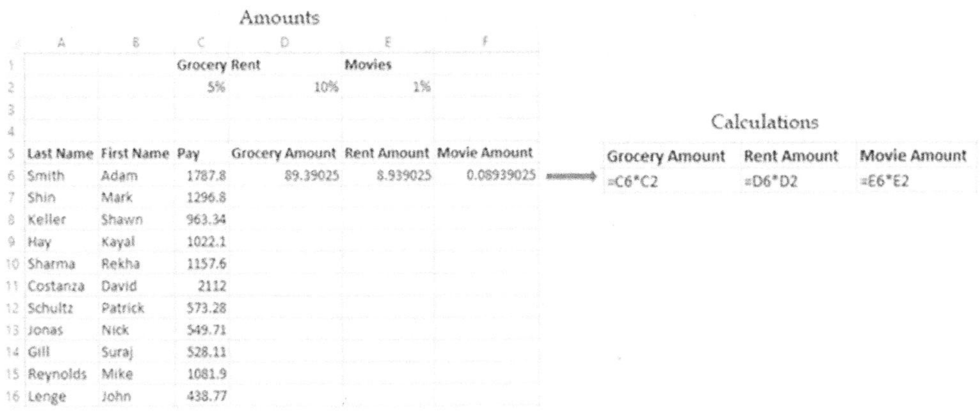

	A	B	C	D	E	F
1			Grocery	Rent	Movies	
2			5%	10%	1%	
3						
4						
5	Last Name	First Name	Pay	Grocery Amount	Rent Amount	Movie Amount
6	Smith	Adam	1787.8	89.39025	8.939025	0.08939025
7	Shin	Mark	1296.8			
8	Keller	Shawn	963.34			
9	Hay	Kayal	1022.1			
10	Sharma	Rekha	1157.6			
11	Costanza	David	2112			
12	Schultz	Patrick	573.28			
13	Jonas	Nick	549.71			
14	Gill	Suraj	528.11			
15	Reynolds	Mike	1081.9			
16	Lenge	John	438.77			

Grocery Amount	Rent Amount	Movie Amount
=C6*C2	=D6*D2	=E6*E2

Figure 3.10: Incorrect results for Rent/Movie Amounts.

What is the reason for the incorrect results?

Notice in the above figure that the Amount and calculation for D6 (Adam Smith Grocery) is correct, but it is incorrect for *Rent* and *Movie*. Due to relative referencing, the *Rent* calculation has changed to D6 * D2 (it should be C6 * D2) and for *Movie,* it has changed to E6 * E2 (it should be C6 * E2). We have to keep the *Pay* (Column C) absolute and row relative.

4. **Resolution.**

   To resolve this issue, delete the previous calculation in D6 and change it to:

```
=$C6*C2
```

   This modification will keep the Pay column (C) constant while allowing the row to change as the formula is copied or auto filled to other cells.

Now, perform autofill horizontally to get the correct amounts for Rent and Movies. The formulas for Rent will appear like =$C6*D2 and for Movies, it will appear as =$C6*E2.

5. **Calculate remaining values.**
   Now, to calculate the values for all the employees, select the cells D6, E6, and F6 and drag them down to autofill in all the cells for different employees.
   This will display incorrect results.

Amounts

Last Name	First Name	Pay	Grocery Amount	Rent Amount	Movie Amount
Smith	Adam	1787.8	89.39025	178.7805	17.87805
Shin	Mark	1296.8	0	0	0
Keller	Shawn	963.34	0	0	0
Hay	Kayal	1022.1	#VALUE!	#VALUE!	#VALUE!
Sharma	Rekha	1157.6	2069559.492	103477.9746	206955.9492
Costanza	David	2112	2738736	0	0
Schultz	Patrick	573.28	552267.6494	0	0
Jonas	Nick	549.71	561852.4164	#VALUE!	#VALUE!
Gill	Suraj	528.11	611339.7165	1092956202	54647810.09
Reynolds	Mike	1081.9	2285015.04	2963093253	0
Lenge	John	438.77	251541.6216	242320105.7	0

Calculations

Grocery Amount	Rent Amount	Movie Amount
=$C6*C2	=$C6*D2	=$C6*E2
=$C7*C3	=$C7*D3	=$C7*E3
=$C8*C4	=$C8*D4	=$C8*E4
=$C9*C5	=$C9*D5	=$C9*E5
=$C10*C6	=$C10*D6	=$C10*E6
=$C11*C7	=$C11*D7	=$C11*E7
=$C12*C8	=$C12*D8	=$C12*E8
=$C13*C9	=$C13*D9	=$C13*E9
=$C14*C10	=$C14*D10	=$C14*E10
=$C15*C11	=$C15*D11	=$C15*E11
=$C16*C12	=$C16*D12	=$C16*E12

Figure 3.11: Incorrect results for rest of the employees.

What is the reason for the incorrect results?
Notice in the above figure, first row for Adam Smith is correct, but in the rest of the rows, the % values are calculated incorrectly. It should consider only C2, D2, and E2, cells but due to relative referencing, it has changed to C3, D3, and E3, etc. in the remaining cells.
In this case, the calculation should keep the row absolute and columns relative.

6. **Resolution.**
   To resolve this issue, delete all the previous calculations. On D6, change the calculation to

```
=$C6*C$2
```

Now, perform autofill horizontally to get the correct amounts for Rent and Movies for Adam Smith. After that, select all the three cells (D6, E6, and F6) and drag them down to autofill the rest of the cells.

The correct output will appear like the one below:

Last Name	First Name	Pay	Grocery Amount	Rent Amount	Movie Amount
Smith	Adam	1787.8	89.39025	178.7805	17.87805
Shin	Mark	1296.8	64.8375	129.675	12.9675
Keller	Shawn	963.34	48.167	96.334	9.6334
Hay	Kayal	1022.1	51.10445	102.2089	10.22089
Sharma	Rekha	1157.6	57.8799	115.7598	11.57598
Costanza	David	2112	105.6	211.2	21.12
Schultz	Patrick	573.28	28.6642125	57.328425	5.7328425
Jonas	Nick	549.71	27.48549375	54.9709875	5.49709875
Gill	Suraj	528.11	26.4055275	52.811055	5.2811055
Reynolds	Mike	1081.9	54.096	108.192	10.8192
Lenge	John	438.77	21.9386475	43.877295	4.3877295

Figure 3.12: Correct results with two types of Mixed referencing.

3-D reference

3-D reference allows referencing cells in multiple worksheets.

- The referenced worksheets should have the same structure.
- It can reference a range of cells and also a range of worksheet names.
- To provide 3-D reference, it must include a cell or a range of cells preceded by a range of worksheet names and an exclamation mark (!).

For e.g., a workbook contains 5 sheets, namely, Sheet1, Sheet2, Sheet3, Sheet4, and Sheet5. Each of these sheets contain a cell for Total (which is stored in cell G5). A 3-D reference can add all of these totals from different sheets. The syntax will be:

```
=Sum(Sheet1:Sheet5!G5)
```

Exercise4: Use the enclosed Chapter3. *IntrotoFormula_2*.xlsx. It has four sheets containing the monthly payroll information for employees. The structure of all the sheets is the same and each one contains a total in Cell C14.

- Calculate the Total of all the months, taking the Totals from Cell C14 in each of the sheets.

Refer to Chapter3. IntrotoFormula_2_Solutions.xlsx for the solution.

Steps to perform 3 – D reference:

1. Open Chapter3.*IntrotoFormula_2*.xlsx and navigate to *All Months Total* sheet.
2. In the cell F5, type the following formula:

   ```
   =SUM(June:Aug!C14)
   ```

   In the formula, June:Aug represents the range of the sheets, and C14 is the cell where the total in each sheet is calculated.

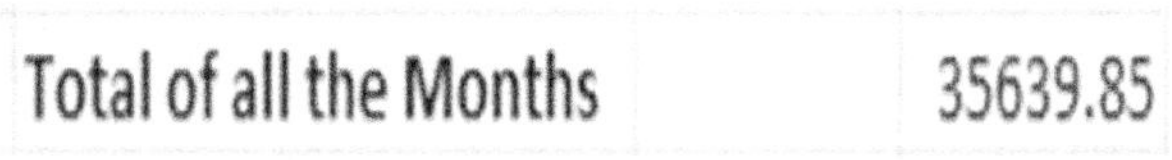

Figure 3.13: Result of 3-D referencing.

R1C1 reference

In Excel, cell addresses can be represented in two ways: A1 style and R1C1 style. In R1C1 reference style:

- Both the row and column of a cell address are referred by a number.
- In A1 style, the first row is denoted by number 1, and the first column is denoted by the letter A. In R1C1 style, both the first row and the first column are represented by R1C1, where both the row and column are referred to by a number.
- By default, Excel uses A1 style. To change to R1C1 style, navigate to File > Options > Formulas and check R1C1 reference style.

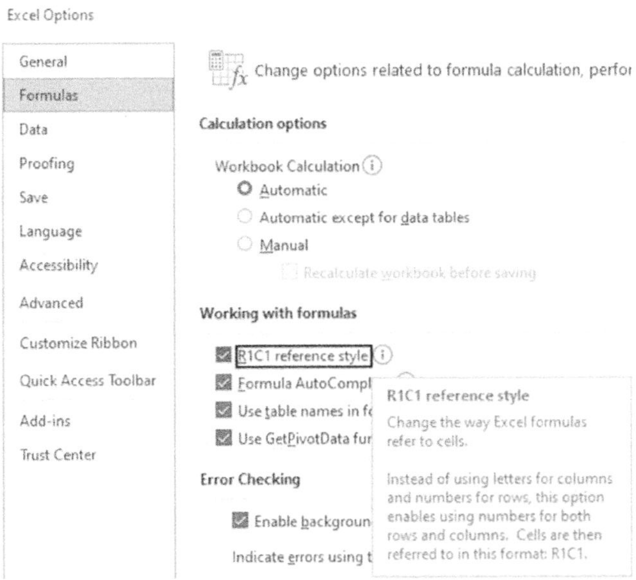

Figure 3.14: Option to change A1 style to R1C1 style.

Difference between A1 style and R1C1 style

In R1C1 style, when referring to any cell in a formula within an active cell, the address of the referred cell is calculated based on its distance from the active cell.

Consider the following example: If a formula (in R1C1 style) refers to the hourly wage of Shawn, the referred address will be R[4]C[2], indicating how far that cell is from the active cell. On the other hand, if we use A1 style, that address will be C5.

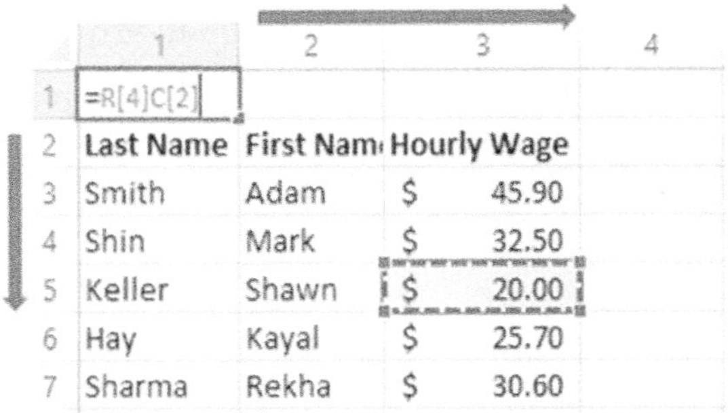

Figure 3.15: Referencing a cell in R1C1 style.

R1C1 style of reference is useful for computing the row and column positions in macros.

Copy values of a Formula

When the cells containing formula are copied and pasted in another sheet, the calculations are also copied which may result in errors because the cell references used in the formula may not be present in the new sheet.

To copy/paste only the values/result of the formula, paste the cells as *values*.

To do this, copy any cell/s containing the formula, go to the destination where these cell values need to be pasted, right-click and select the *Paste Options,* and then *Paste Special*. In the subsequent dialog box, select *Values*.

Figure 3.16: Copy and Paste values of a formula.

The *Paste Special* in the Pasting Options will be useful when only values are required to be copied and not the actual formula.

Chapter 4
Logical Functions

The previous chapter provided an introduction to formulas and how to use cell references. This chapter will explain the usage of Logical functions. Logical functions are a powerful set of tools that allow performing logical tests on data and making decisions based on the results.

The following topics will be discussed in this chapter:

- Overview of Logical Functions
- The IF function
- Nested IF and IFS
- The AND function
- The OR function
- The NOT function
- The IFERROR function

Overview of Logical Functions

Logical functions in Excel test a condition, which can be an expression or a value. This condition evaluates to True or False. Based on the result (True or False), an action can be performed which can again be a value or an expression.

Whenever users need to perform an action based on a condition, logical functions come into play. These functions can be nested or used with other functions to create complex logic.
Excel provides a wide variety of Logical functions. The subsequent sections will explain each of these functions.

The IF function

The IF function was already introduced in the earlier chapter. It evaluates a logical expression and displays one value if the condition is true and another value if the condition is false.

Syntax:

=IF (logical_test, value_if_True, value_if_false)

Where:

The logical_test is the condition that is tested to determine if it is true or false. If the condition is true, the function returns the value specified in the value_if_true argument; otherwise, it returns the value specified in the value_if_false argument.

The logical_test can perform tests on numbers or text values, making it a versatile and powerful function for decision-making in Excel.

Exercise1: Use the enclosed Chapter4.LogicalFunctions.xlsx to perform this exercise.

In the blank column K (High/Regular), perform the following calculation:

- If Sales are greater than 500, label them as *High;* otherwise, label them as *Regular*.

Refer to Chapter4.LogicalFunctions_Solutions.xlsx for the solution.

Steps to use the IF function:

1. Open Chapter4_LogicalFunctions.xlsx. Work on the same sheet or create a copy of it.
2. Go to Column K (High/Regular).
   - Click on cell K2, type "=", and then type *IF*. Press *Tab* on the keyboard. It will display = *IF(* . The syntax of the calculation will also be shown.
   - Select Column J2 (Sales) and type the calculation as

```
=IF(J2>500,"High","Regular")
```

This calculation will evaluate the condition *J2>500;* if it is true, "High" will be displayed; otherwise "Regular" will be displayed.

3. After the first value is displayed correctly, drag it down to autofill the rest of the cells.

Sales		High/Regular
$	475.94	Regular
$	411.33	Regular
$	11.85	Regular
$	795.41	High
$	13.36	Regular
$	129.89	Regular
$	310.69	Regular
$	567.12	High
$	187.76	Regular
$	1,125.49	High
$	16.28	Regular
$	25.16	Regular
$	173.94	Regular
$	239.98	Regular
$	836.59	High
$	7.04	Regular
$	370.62	Regular
$	11.23	Regular

Figure 4.1: Result of the IF function.

The IF function is the key logical function that can be used in different scenarios.

Nested IF and IFS

The previously explained IF function can only perform one logical test. The Nested IF function can perform multiple logical tests by nesting one IF function inside another.

Syntax:

=IF(logical_test1, value_if_true1,IF(logical_test2, value_if_true2,IF(logical_test3, value_if_true3, value_if_false3)))

The IFS function is a newer addition in Excel 2016. It is much cleaner than Nested IF and produces the same result.

Syntax:

IFS(condition1, value1, [condition2, value2], ...)

Exercise2: Use the enclosed Chapter4.LogicalFunctions.xlsx to perform this exercise.
Perform the calculation to provide various incentives based on the segment. Use both Nested IF and IFS functions:

- If Segment = "Home Office", give an incentive of $2, if Segment = "Corporate", give an incentive of $3, and if Segment = "Consumer", give an incentive of $4.
  Since multiple conditions need to be checked, we can use a Nested IF.

Refer to Chapter4.LogicalFunctions_Solutions.xlsx for the solution.

Steps to use the Nested IF function:

1. Use the same workbook as used in the previous exercise.
2. Go to Column T/ Nested IF (Cell T2) and type the formula as shown below:

```
=IF(G2="Home
Office","$2",IF(G2="Corporate","$3",IF(G2="Consumer","$4
")))
```

3. After the first value is displayed correctly, drag it down to autofill the rest of the cells.
4. Using IFS function.
   Go to Column U/IFS (cell U2) and type the formula as shown below:

```
=IFS(G2 = "Home Office","$2",G2 = "Corporate","$3",G2 =
"Consumer","$4")
```

This formula will produce the same result as Nested IF.

The AND function

The AND function, as the name suggests, compares more than one condition. It returns True if all the conditions are satisfied; otherwise returns False.

Syntax:

=AND(Condition1, Condition2…)

The condition in the function can perform a test on a number or a text. The AND function can also be used with IF.

Exercise3: Use the enclosed Chapter4.LogicalFunctions.xlsx to perform this exercise.
Type the formula in the blank *Column L* (Bonus decision).
The management wants to decide the bonus based on the following condition:

- If Sales is greater 600 and the Region is not West, then display "Bonus is 20%"; otherwise display "TBD".

Since we need to check for two conditions, the AND function will be used.

Refer to Chapter4.LogicalFunctions_Solutions.xlsx for the solution.

Steps to use the AND function:

1. Use the previous sheet and navigate to Column L (Bonus Decision).
2. In Cell L2, type the following formula using the function AND function:

```
AND(J2>600, H2<>"West")
```

This formula will return "True" if the Sales (Column J2) is greater than 600 and Region (Column H2) is not equal to West.

3. Autofill the remaining cells in Column L. It will display True for three cells, and the rest will be False.
4. Use AND with IF.
   Modify the calculation on L2 to include the AND function within the IF function.

   ```
   =IF(AND(J2>600, H2<>"West"),"20% Bonus","TBD")
   ```

   In the above IF function, the AND function is used as a logical test. If it evaluates to true, it returns "20% Bonus"; otherwise, it returns false, returns "TBD".
5. Autofill the rest of Column L with this new calculation.

Bonus Decision
TBD
TBD
TBD
20% Bonus
TBD
TBD
TBD
TBD
TBD
20% Bonus
TBD
TBD
TBD
TBD
20% Bonus
TBD
TBD
TBD

Figure 4.2: Result of using IF with the AND function.

The AND function can be used in various scenarios, such as checking multiple criteria before performing an action, validating data, and creating complex logical expressions.

The OR function

The OR function compares more than one condition. It returns true if *ANY* of the conditions are satisfied, otherwise returns false.

Syntax:

=OR(Condition1, Condition2…)

The condition in the function can perform a test on numbers or a text. The OR function can also be used with IF.

Exercise4: Use the enclosed Chapter4.LogicalFunctions.xlsx to perform this exercise.
Type the formula on the blank *Column M* (Shipping Charge).
The management wants to decide when to charge customer for Shipping based on the following condition:

- If Ship Mode is "Priority Delivery" or Sales is less than $100, display "Shipping Charge"; otherwise display "No Shipping Charge".

Since we need to check either of the two conditions, OR function will be used.

Refer to Chapter4.LogicalFunctions_Solutions.xlsx for the solution.

Steps to use the OR function:

1. Use the previous sheet and navigate to Column M (Shipping Charge?).
2. In Cell M2, type the formula using the OR function

```
=OR(D2="Priority delivery",J2<100)
```

This formula will return "True" if either the *Ship Mode* (Column D2) is "Priority Delivery" or *Sales* (Column J2) is less than 100.
The calculation on cell M2 will return True as one condition (Ship Mode = Priority) is true.

3. Autofill the remaining cells of Column M with this formula. Based on the condition specified in the formula, several Trues and Falses will be displayed.
4. Use OR with IF.
   Modify the calculation on M2 to enclose the OR function within the IF function.

```
=IF(OR(D2="Priority        delivery",J2<100),"Shipping
Charge", "No Shipping Charge")
```

In the above IF function, the OR function is used as a logical test. If it is true, it returns "Shipping Charge", if false, returns "No Shipping Charge".

Ship Mode	Sales	Shipping Charge ?
Priority Delivery	$ 475.94	Shipping Charge
Standard Freight	$ 411.33	No Shipping Charge
Priority Delivery	$ 11.85	Shipping Charge
Second Class	$ 795.41	No Shipping Charge
Priority Delivery	$ 13.36	Shipping Charge
Priority Delivery	$ 129.89	Shipping Charge
Standard Freight	$ 310.69	No Shipping Charge
Priority Delivery	$ 567.12	Shipping Charge
First Class	$ 187.76	No Shipping Charge
Priority Delivery	$ 1,125.49	Shipping Charge
Priority Delivery	$ 16.28	Shipping Charge
Priority Delivery	$ 25.16	Shipping Charge
Standard Freight	$ 173.94	No Shipping Charge
Priority Delivery	$ 239.98	Shipping Charge
Standard Freight	$ 836.59	No Shipping Charge
Second Class	$ 7.04	Shipping Charge
First Class	$ 370.62	No Shipping Charge
Standard Freight	$ 11.23	Shipping Charge

Figure 4.3: Result of using IF with OR function.

Verify the calculation against the results with Ship Mode and Sales. Check if the "Shipping Charge" or "No Shipping Charge" is displayed correctly based on the specified conditions in the OR function.

The NOT function

The Not function reverses the behavior of the IF function. It always returns the opposite logical value. It returns true if false is provided and returns false if true is provided.

Syntax:

=Not (Condition)

Exercise5: Use the enclosed Chapter4.LogicalFunctions.xlsx to perform this exercise.

Type the formula in the blank column N (High/Regular using NOT) and O (NOT with multiple values).

- Perform the calculation to achieve the same functionality as done in High/Regular using the IF function in Exercise 1.
- Use the NOT function to check for multiple values.

Refer to Chapter4.LogicalFunctions_Solutions.xlsx for the solution.

Steps to use the NOT function:

1. Continue using the previous sheet and navigate to Column N (High/Regular using NOT).
2. In the Cell N2, type the formula using the NOT function

```
=IF(NOT(J2>500),"Regular","High")
```

   Notice that it uses the reverse of the earlier *IF* function (specified in Exercise 1). The *NOT* function checks if Sales in *not* greater than 500 and uses the IF function to display Regular and High.
3. Autofill the remaining cells in Column N. It will produce the same result as in Column K.
4. Using NOT to check multiple values.
   To use NOT for checking multiple values, use it in conjunction with AND or OR function.
   - On *Cell 02* (NOT with multiple values), type the calculation as:

```
=IF(NOT(AND(G2="Home Office",H2="West")),J2,0)
```

This calculation will check if Segment is not "Home Office" and Region (H2) is not "West", then displays Sales(J2), else displays 0.

High/Regular using NOT	NOT with multiple
Regular	$0.00
Regular	$0.00
Regular	$11.85
High	$795.41
Regular	$13.36
Regular	$129.89
Regular	$310.69
High	$567.12
Regular	$0.00
High	$1,125.49
Regular	$16.28
Regular	$25.16
Regular	$173.94
Regular	$239.98
High	$836.59
Regular	$7.04
Regular	$370.62
Regular	$11.23

Figure 4.4: Result of NOT function.

The NOT function offers flexibility and enhances the capabilities of Excel when dealing with various data scenarios.

The IFERROR function

The IFERROR function is used to handle errors in Excel and is designed to catch and manage errors in a formula.

Syntax:

=IFERROR (Value, Value_if_Error)

Exercise6: Use the enclosed Chapter4.LogicalFunctions.xlsx to perform this exercise.
Type the formula in the blank column P (IFERROR).

- Divide Column J (Sales) with Column R (Discount) to intentionally produce a divide by 0 error. Now, resolve the error using IFERROR.

Refer to Chapter4.LogicalFunctions_Solutions.xlsx for the solution.

Steps to use the IFERROR function:

1. Continue using the previous sheet and navigate to Column P (IFERROR).
2. In Cell P2, type the formula:

```
=J2/R2
```

3. Autofill the remaining cells in *Column P*. Notice the error *#DIV/0!*; it is a divide-by-0 error as some of the discount values are 0%.

IFError
$2,379.72
$2,742.21
#DIV/0!
$3,977.04
#DIV/0!
$649.44
$1,553.44
$2,835.60
#DIV/0!
$5,627.44
#DIV/0!
$41.93
#DIV/0!
#DIV/0!
$2,091.48
#DIV/0!
$926.55

Figure 4.5: Divide by zero error.

4. This error can be fixed by using the IFERROR function.

Delete all the values in Column P and modify the calculation in cell P2 with the following formula:

```
=IFERROR(J2/R2,0)
```

The IFERROR function will display 0 in case of an error.

IFError
$2,379.72
$2,742.21
$0.00
$3,977.04
$0.00
$649.44
$1,553.44
$2,835.60
$0.00
$5,627.44
$0.00
$41.93
$0.00
$0.00
$2,091.48
$0.00
$926.55
$56.16

Figure 4.6: The IFERROR function displays 0 instead of an error.

The IFERROR function in Excel is a valuable tool for handling errors that may occur in formulas. It provides a way to catch and manage errors, ensuring that the spreadsheet remains accurate and functional even in the presence of errors.

Chapter 5
Text Functions

The previous chapter provided an explanation on Logical functions and how to use them in checking conditions in a calculation. This chapter will explore the use of Text functions in Excel. Text functions help in extracting specific parts of a text, combine text from different cells, finding the length of text, remove unwanted characters, and much more.

The following topics will be discussed in this chapter:

- Overview of Text Functions
- The LEFT, RIGHT, and MID functions
- The LEN function
- The CONCAT function

Overview of Text Functions

The Text functions, also called String functions, are used in manipulating strings in Excel. String values include data such as, names, Addresses, and more.

Some of the useful string functions are:

- The LEFT, Right and MID functions
- The LEN function
- The CONCAT function

The following sections will explain each of these functions in detail.

The LEFT, RIGHT, and MID function

The Left, Right, and Mid functions are used to extract a specified number of characters from a given string.

The LEFT function

The LEFT function returns the specified number of characters from the left of the string.

Syntax:

=LEFT (Text, number of characters)

Where:

The text or string from which the user wants to extract characters. The number of characters is optional and specifies the number of characters to be extracted from the left or the start of the string. If omitted, it will return the first letter from the left.

The RIGHT function

The RIGHT function is similar to LEFT but starts from the right-side of the string. It returns the specified number of characters of the string from the right.

Syntax:

=RIGHT (Text, number of characters)

Where:

The text or string from which the user wants to extract characters. The number of characters is optional and specifies the characters to extract from the right side of the text.

The MID function

The MID function is used to extract a specified number of characters from a string, starting at the specified position and number of characters to be extracted.

Syntax:

=MID (Text, start_num, num_chars)

Where:

The text or string from which the user wants to extract characters. The start_num provides the position from which the extraction should begin. Num_chars signifies the number of characters to be extracted from the text.

Exercise1: Use the enclosed Chapter5.TextFunctions.xlsx to perform this exercise.

The Order ID (Column B) is a combination of Country, Year, and Order Number. The objective is to split these string values into different columns:

- Extract the string 'US' from *Order ID*. Type this formula in Column C (Country).
- Extract Order number from the *Order ID*. Type this formula in Column D (Order Number).
- Extract Year from the *Order ID*. Type this formula in Column E (Year).

Refer to Chapter5.TextFunctions_Solutions.xlsx for the solution.

Steps to use the LEFT, RIGHT and MID functions:

1. Open Chapter5.TextFunctions.xlsx. Work on the same sheet or make a copy of it.
2. LEFT function.
   Navigate to Column C (Country).
   - Click on cell C2, type "=" and then type *LEFT*. Press tab on the keyboard. It will display = *LEFT(* . The syntax of the calculation will also be displayed.
   - Select Column B2 (Order ID) and type the calculation as

```
=LEFT(B2,2)
```

   This calculation will start from the left side of Order ID and extract 2 characters.

3. After the first value is displayed correctly, drag it down to autofill the rest of the cells.
4. RIGHT function.
   Navigate to Column D (Order Number) and type the calculation on cell D2:

   ```
   =RIGHT(B2,6)
   ```

   This formula will start from the right and will extract 6 characters. Autofill the rest of the cells.
5. MID Function.
   Navigate to Column E (Year) and type the calculation on cell E2:

   ```
   =MID(B2,4,4)
   ```

   This formula will start from the position 4 and return 4 characters.

   After implementing all the three functions, the result will appear as below:

Order ID	Country	Order Number	Year
US-2021-133949	US	133949	2021
US-2021-105249	US	105249	2021
US-2021-113047	US	113047	2021
US-2021-141649	US	141649	2021
US-2021-135699	US	135699	2021
US-2021-131541	US	131541	2021
US-2021-152254	US	152254	2021
US-2021-124429	US	124429	2021
US-2021-120740	US	120740	2021
US-2021-130428	US	130428	2021
US-2021-129609	US	129609	2021
US-2021-165589	US	165589	2021
US-2022-160304	US	160304	2022
US-2022-108504	US	108504	2022
US-2022-143819	US	143819	2022
US-2022-127985	US	127985	2022
US-2022-164784	US	164784	2022
US-2022-119046	US	119046	2022

Figure 5.1: Result of Left, Right, and Mid functions.

The LEN function

The LEN or length function returns the length of a string or the number of characters in a string. It counts the special characters and spaces in the string. It works on dates and numbers too but does not count the formatting portion.

Syntax:

LEN (TEXT)

Exercise2: Use the enclosed Chapter5.TextFunctions.xlsx to perform this exercise.

- Find the length of the *Order Number* (Column D). Place this value in *Column F* (Length of Order Number).
- Find the length of the *Order Date* (Column G). Place this value in *Column H* (Length of Order Date).
- Find the length of the *Sales* (Column O). Place this value in Column P (Length of Sales)

Refer to Chapter5.TextFunctions_Solutions.xlsx for the solution.

Steps to use the LEN function:

1. Continue working on the previous sheet.
2. Finding the length of a string
   Navigate to *Column F* and type the formula in cell F2:

   ```
   =LEN(D2)
   ```

   This will calculate the length of the *Order Number* stored in Cell D2. Autofill the rest of the cells in Column D
3. Finding the length of a Date.
   Navigate to *Column H* and type the formula as on cell H2:

   ```
   =LEN(G2)
   ```

   This will calculate the length of *Order Date* stored in Cell G2. Autofill the rest of the cells in Column H.

Notice that Excel avoided the data formatting characters (/) while calculating the length of date.

4. Finding the length of a Number.
   Navigate to *Column P* and type the formula as on cell P2:

```
=LEN(O2)
```

This will calculate the length of *Sales* stored in Cell G2. Autofill the rest to the cells in Column P.

Notice Excel considers the $ sign and space while calculating the length of the number.

Length of Order Number	Length of Order Date	Length of Sales
6	5	7
6	5	7
6	5	5
6	5	7
6	5	5
6	5	7
6	5	7
6	5	6
6	5	6
6	5	8
6	5	5
6	5	5
6	5	6
6	5	6
6	5	7
6	5	4
6	5	6
6	5	6

Figure 5.2: Result of the LEN function.

Utility of LEN function

LEN function can be used in conjunction with other functions to track errors or enforce specific business rules. For example, according to a business rule, Order Number should always be 6 characters long. A calculation can be created to check this:

```
=IF(LEN(D2) > 6, "Incorrect", "Correct")
```

In this way, Order numbers having length greater than 6 will be marked as "Incorrect".

The CONCAT function

The CONCAT function combines text from different cells or a range of cells. It replaces the CONCATENATE function, although the CONCATENATE function is still available.

Syntax:

CONCAT (TEXT1,TEXT2…)

Text1, Text2 are the strings to be concatenated.

Exercise3: Use the enclosed Chapter5.TextFunctions.xlsx to perform this exercise.

- Create a new Order ID column which should combine the fields Order Number, Year, and first three letters of Region in upper case. The new Order ID will appear in the format 133949-2021-WES

This exercise will also use the UPPER function which will convert a string to upper case letters.

Refer to Chapter5.TextFunctions_Solutions.xlsx for the solution.

Steps to use the CONCAT function:

1. Continue working on the previous sheet.
2. Navigate to Column T (New Order ID) and on cell T2, type the following formula:

```
=CONCAT(D2,"-”,E2,"-",UPPER(LEFT(M2,3)))
```

The formula will work as follows:

- Select D2
- Concatenate it with "-"
- Select E2
- Concatenate it with "-"
- The LEFT (M2,3) will take three letters of Region from the left and use UPPER to convert them to upper case letters.
- Finally, CONCAT will concatenate all the strings present in the calculation.

3. Autofill the rest of the cells on Column T.

New Order ID
133949-2021-WES
105249-2021-WES
113047-2021-SOU
141649-2021-EAS
135699-2021-WES
131541-2021-SOU
152254-2021-SOU
124429-2021-WES
120740-2021-WES
130428-2021-SOU
129609-2021-CEN
165589-2021-CEN
160304-2022-EAS
108504-2022-SOU
143819-2022-EAS
127985-2022-SOU
164784-2022-SOU
119046-2022-WES

Figure 5.3: Result of CONCAT function.

The CONCAT function allows users to create new text strings by joining multiple text values without the need for complex formulas or manual string manipulation.

Chapter 6
DateTime Functions

The previous chapter provided an explanation on Text functions and how to use them to perform operations on string values. This chapter will explore the use of DateTime functions. These functions enable users to perform tasks like calculating the difference between two dates, extracting the day, month, or year from a date, adding or subtracting time intervals, and converting date formats.

The following topics will be discussed in this chapter:

- Overview of Dates
- Adding or subtracting days from dates
- The EDATE function
- The DATE, YEAR, MONTH, and DAY functions
- Calculating Quarters
- TODAY, NOW, and TIME functions
- NETWORKDAYS function

Overview of Dates

Dates are essential for data storage and analysis as they help in tracking the data by dates.

- In an Excel cell, a date is stored as a serial number, but the cell formatting displays it in the date format.
- The time portion present in the date is represented as decimals.
- Dates stored as serial numbers allow performing numerical calculations on dates.
- The default date format is m/d/yyyy. Excel dates start from January 1, 1900 and the serial number of the date '1/1/1900' is 1, '1/2/1900' is 2, and so on.

- The date format and serial number can be checked by typing 1, 2, etc. in any cell and formatting it to date.
- Dates can be formatted in different ways by using *Format Cells.*
- When filters are applied, an aggregated date format is displayed.

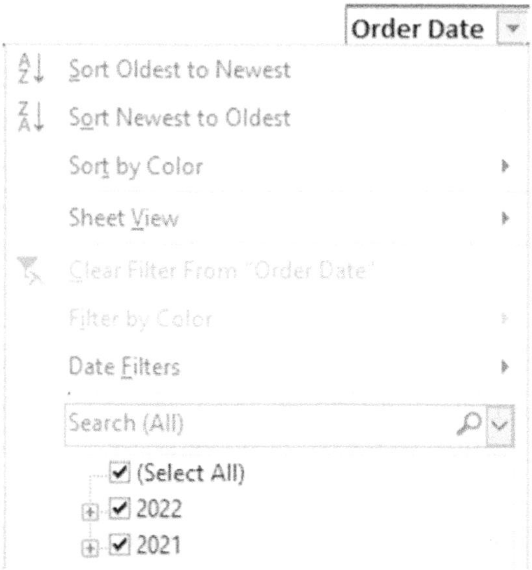

Figure 6.1: Dates aggregated to Years in filters.

Excel provides a number of useful date functions that allow performing date-level calculations.

Add or subtract days from dates

Since dates are stored as serial numbers, users can add or subtract days from dates using normal mathematical operation.

Exercise1: Use the enclosed Chapter6.DateTimeFunctions.xlsx to perform this exercise.

- Calculate *Sales Call Date,* which is seven days prior to the *Order Date*
- Calculate *Survey Date,* which is three days from the Order Date

Refer to Chapter6.DateTimeFunctions_Solutions.xlsx for the solution.

Steps to Add or subtract days from dates:

1. Open Chapter6.*DateTimeFunctions*.xlsx. Work on the same sheet or make a copy of it.
2. Navigate to Column C (Sales Call Date)
   - Click on cell C2, type "=" and then select cell D2 (Order Date), add minus sign "-" and type 7. The formula should appear like:

```
= D2-7
```

3. After the first value is displayed correctly, drag it down to autofill the rest of the cells.
4. Navigate to Column G (Survey Date).
   - Click on cell G2, type "=" and then select cell D2 (Order Date), add plus (+) and type 3. The formula should appear like

```
= D2+3
```

5. After the first value is displayed correctly, drag it down to autofill the rest of the cells.

After performing the calculation, the dates will appear as below:

C	D	E	F	G
Sales Call Date	Order Date	Ship Mode	Ship Date	Survey Date
12/25/2020	1/1/2021	Priority Delivery	1/2/2021	1/4/2021
1/25/2021	2/1/2021	Standard Freight	2/10/2021	2/4/2021
2/22/2021	3/1/2021	Priority Delivery	3/2/2021	3/4/2021
3/25/2021	4/1/2021	Second Class	4/7/2021	4/4/2021
4/24/2021	5/1/2021	Priority Delivery	5/2/2021	5/4/2021
5/25/2021	6/1/2021	Priority Delivery	6/2/2021	6/4/2021
6/24/2021	7/1/2021	Standard Freight	7/10/2021	7/4/2021
7/25/2021	8/1/2021	Priority Delivery	8/2/2021	8/4/2021
8/25/2021	9/1/2021	First Class	9/4/2021	9/4/2021
9/24/2021	10/1/2021	Priority Delivery	10/2/2021	10/4/2021
10/25/2021	11/1/2021	Priority Delivery	11/2/2021	11/4/2021
11/24/2021	12/1/2021	Priority Delivery	12/2/2021	12/4/2021
12/25/2021	1/1/2022	Standard Freight	1/10/2022	1/4/2022
1/25/2022	2/1/2022	Priority Delivery	2/2/2022	2/4/2022
2/22/2022	3/1/2022	Standard Freight	3/10/2022	3/4/2022
3/25/2022	4/1/2022	Second Class	4/7/2022	4/4/2022
4/24/2022	5/1/2022	First Class	5/4/2022	5/4/2022
5/25/2022	6/1/2022	Standard Freight	6/10/2022	6/4/2022

Figure 6.2: Add or subtract days from Dates.

The EDATE function

The EDATE function is used to add or subtract months from a date.

Syntax:

=EDATE (start_date, months)

Where:

Start_date is the date to which the number of months needs to be added. To add months, provide a positive number and to subtract months, provide a negative number for the *months* attribute.

Exercise2: Use the enclosed Chapter6.*DateTimeFunctions*.xlsx to perform this exercise.

- Calculate *Payment Date,* which is 3 months from the *Order Date.*

  Refer to Chapter6.DateTimeFunctions_Solutions.xlsx for the solution.

Steps to use EDATE function:

1. Continue working on the same sheet used in the previous exercise.
2. Navigate to Column H (Payment Date)
   - Click on cell H2, type "=" and then type the function EDATE. Press *Tab* on the keyboard. This will display opening parenthesis and the syntax of the function.
   - Select cell D2 (Order Date) and type comma ",", and then type 3. The formula should appear as

     ```
     =EDATE(D2,3)
     ```

3. After the first value is displayed correctly, drag it down to autofill the rest of the cells.

Order Date	Payment Date
1/1/2021	4/1/2021
2/1/2021	5/1/2021
3/1/2021	6/1/2021
4/1/2021	7/1/2021
5/1/2021	8/1/2021
6/1/2021	9/1/2021
7/1/2021	10/1/2021
8/1/2021	11/1/2021
9/1/2021	12/1/2021
10/1/2021	1/1/2022
11/1/2021	2/1/2022
12/1/2021	3/1/2022
1/1/2022	4/1/2022
2/1/2022	5/1/2022
3/1/2022	6/1/2022
4/1/2022	7/1/2022
5/1/2022	8/1/2022
6/1/2022	9/1/2022

Figure 6.3: Adding Dates using EDATE.

To subtract a specific number of months from the date, use a negative number in the calculation.

The DATE, YEAR, MONTH, and DAY functions

The Date, Year, Month, and Day functions are useful in creating a date.

The DATE function

The DATE function returns the sequential serial number that represents a specific date based on the provided Year, Month, and Day arguments.

Syntax:

=DATE (year, month, day)

Where:

Year can include 4 digits. Month can include an integer representing 1to 12 months in a year. Day can include an integer representing the day of the month from 1 to 31.

The YEAR function

The YEAR function returns the Year of the provided date. The year is returned as an integer between 1900 through 9999. If the resulting cell does not display the correct year, make sure that its format is General or number.

Syntax:

=YEAR (serial number)

Where:

Serial number is the date of the year.

The MONTH function

The MONTH function returns the month of the provided date as an integer ranging from 1 - 12.

Syntax:

=Month (serial number)

Where:

Serial number is the date of the year.

The DAY function

The DAY function returns the day of the provided date as an integer ranging from 1 - 31.

Syntax:

=DAY (serial number)

Where:

Serial number is the date of the year.

Tip: If after applying the formula, the resulting cell does not display the correct year or month, make sure that its format is *General* or *Number* with no decimal places.

Exercise3: Use the enclosed Chapter6.*DateTimeFunctions*.xlsx to perform this exercise.

The requirement is to remind the customers to re-order the products after one year, two months and fifteen days from the order date.

To perform this:

- Calculate *Reorder call* by adding one year, 2 months, and 15 days to the *Order Date*

  Refer to Chapter6.DateTimeFunctions_Solutions.xlsx for the solution.

Steps to use Year, Month, and Day functions:

1. Continue working on the same sheet used in the previous exercise. This exercise will involve using the DATE function by providing Year, Month, and Day values. Recall the syntax of DATE, which is =DATE (year, month, day)
2. Navigate to *Column I* (Reorder Call)
   - Click on cell I2, type "=" and then type the function DATE. Press *Tab* on the keyboard. This will display opening parenthesis and the syntax of the function.
   - Type YEAR and press *Tab*, select *D2* and add (+1) to it. Type a "," after this.
   - Type MONTH and press *Tab*, select *D2* and add (+2) to it. Type a "," after this.
   - Type DAY and press *Tab*, select *D2* and add (+15) to it. Type a "," after this.
   - Close the parenthesis and press *Enter*.
   - The formula should appear as:

```
=DATE(YEAR(D2) + 1,MONTH(D2) + 2,DAY(D2)+15)
```

3. After the first value is displayed correctly, drag it down to autofill the rest of the cells.

Order Date	Reorder Call
1/1/2021	3/16/2022
2/1/2021	4/16/2022
3/1/2021	5/16/2022
4/1/2021	6/16/2022
5/1/2021	7/16/2022
6/1/2021	8/16/2022
7/1/2021	9/16/2022
8/1/2021	10/16/2022
9/1/2021	11/16/2022
10/1/2021	12/16/2022
11/1/2021	1/16/2023
12/1/2021	2/16/2023
1/1/2022	3/16/2023
2/1/2022	4/16/2023
3/1/2022	5/16/2023
4/1/2022	6/16/2023
5/1/2022	7/16/2023
6/1/2022	8/16/2023

Figure 6.4: Result of Date, Year, Month, and Day functions.

By using these functions, users can easily perform calculations based on years, months, and days, enabling them to keep track of time-related data with precision.

Calculating Quarters

Calculating Quarters in Excel requires using the MONTH and ROUNDUP functions. Excel does not have a direct function to calculate a Quarter, so it is derived from the MONTH and ROUNDUP functions.

The ROUNDUP function is used to always round up to the nearest number of decimal places.

Syntax:

=*ROUNDUP (number, num_digits)*

Where:

Number is the number to be rounded up and num_digits is the number of decimal places to which the number should be rounded up.

For example, =ROUNDUP(67.57,1) will round up the number to 67.6, and =ROUNDUP(67.57,0) will round up the number to 68.

Exercise4: Use the enclosed Chapter6.*DateTimeFunctions*.xlsx to perform this exercise.

- Find the quarters of the *Order Date.*

  Refer to Chapter6.DateTimeFunctions_Solutions.xlsx for the solution.

Steps to find the Quarter:

1. Continue working on the same sheet used in the previous exercise.
2. Navigate to Column J (Order Date Quarters).
   - On Cell J2, type "=" and then ROUNDUP, press the *Tab* key on the keyboard.
   - To supply the number to the ROUNDUP function, type "MONTH(" and either type D2 or select the cell D2 and type "/3".
   - Type "," , and type 0. This will roundup the number to 0 places of decimals.

     The resulting formula will appear as:

```
=ROUNDUP(MONTH(D2)/3,0)
```

3. After the first value is displayed correctly, drag it down to autofill the rest of the cells.

   This will provide the quarters from the Order Date.

Order Date	Order Date Quarters
1/1/2021	1
2/1/2021	1
3/1/2021	1
4/1/2021	2
5/1/2021	2
6/1/2021	2
7/1/2021	3
8/1/2021	3
9/1/2021	3
10/1/2021	4
11/1/2021	4
12/1/2021	4
1/1/2022	1
2/1/2022	1
3/1/2022	1
4/1/2022	2
5/1/2022	2
6/1/2022	2

Figure 6.5: Quarters from Order Date.

The combination of MONTH and ROUNDUP functions can be used efficiently to determine the quarters of specific dates.

TODAY, NOW, and TIME functions

The Today, Now, and Time functions enable users to display the current date, current date and time, and create custom time values.

TODAY and NOW functions

The TODAY and NOW functions are used to display the system date. These dates will always reflect the current system date when the excel workbook is opened on any given day.

Syntax:

=TODAY ()

=NOW ()

TODAY returns the current date formatted as date.

NOW returns the current date and time formatted as date and time.

The difference between TODAY and NOW is that the former returns only the date and the latter returns the date with time.

Tip: Time value can be added or subtracted from system date NOW() by proving the decimal value. For example, to add half a day, simply use =NOW() + .5

The TIME function

The TIME function creates a time with the provided hours, minutes, and seconds.

Syntax:

=TIME(hour, minute, second)

Exercise5: Use the enclosed Chapter6.*DateTimeFunctions*.xlsx to perform this exercise.

- Create a formula to add 15 hours, 20 mins and 30 secs to the system date.

  Refer to Chapter6. DateTimeFunctions_Solutions.xlsx (Sheet Now) for the solution.

Steps to use NOW function:

1. Use the sheet named *NOW* in the same workbook.
2. Navigate to D4 and type the following formula:

```
=NOW() + TIME(5,20,30)
```

In the above formula, NOW() will provide the system's date and TIME function will add the hours, minutes, and seconds to it.

NETWORKDAYS function

The NETWORKDAYS function in Excel is used to calculate the number of working days between two specified start and end dates, excluding weekends and specified holidays. It includes both the start date and end dates in the calculation. This function is useful for calculating the number of days while excluding non-working days.

Syntax:
=NETWORKDAYS(start_date,end_date,[holidays])
Where:
Start_date. The start date in the range.
End_date. The end date in the range.
Holidays. Optional. A list of dates that are considered holidays and should be excluded from the count. A range of cells containing the holiday dates must be provided.

Exercise6: Use the enclosed Chapter6.*DateTimeFunctions*.xlsx to perform this exercise.

- Find the working days between Order Date and Ship Date.

  Refer to Chapter6. DateTimeFunctions_Solutions.xlsx (Sheet Now) for the solution.

Steps to use NETWORKDAYS function:

1. Use the sheet named *Sheet1* in the same workbook.
2. Navigate to Column S/ Network Days (Cell S2) and type the following formula:

```
=NETWORKDAYS (D2,F2)
```

3. After the first value is displayed correctly, drag it down to autofill the rest of the cells.
   This will provide the working days between the two dates.

Chapter 7
Mathematical Functions

The previous chapter explained DateTime functions and their application in date calculations. In this chapter, the focus is on the essential Mathematical and Statistical functions in Excel, specifically delving into aggregation functions like COUNT and SUM.

The following topics will be discussed in this chapter:

- COUNT functions
- SUM, SUMIF, and SUMIFS functions

The Mathematical functions in Excel perform mathematical computations on a group/range of cells. Excel provides a wide range of such functions. The subsequent sections will explain the use these mathematical functions.

The COUNT functions

Excel provides various Count functions, such as COUNT, COUNTA, and COUNTIF.

COUNT function

The COUNT function counts the cells that contain numbers, dates, and numbers formatted as Text. It does not count the blank cells, error values, text values, and logical values.

Syntax:

=COUNT(value1, value2..)

It can also accept a range of cells, for example, =Count(A2:A10)

COUNTA function

The COUNTA function is similar to COUNT but can count error values, text, and logical values in a cell. It does not count the blank cells.

COUNTIF function

The COUNTIF function counts only the cells that meet a certain criterion.

Syntax:

=COUNTIF(range, criteria)

Where:

Range is the range of cells and criteria is the condition specified in double quotes. For example, = COUNTIF(A2:A10, “>5”)

Exercise1: Use the enclosed Chapter7.MathematicalFunctions.xlsx (Sheet Counts) to perform this exercise.

The provided data contains a set of values in a combination of numbers, dates, blanks, numbers formatted as text, errors, and text value.

- Calculate *COUNT, COUNTA, and COUNTIF* using the provided values to see the difference in the resulting values.

  Refer to Chapter7.MathematicalFunctions_Solutions.xlsx (Sheet Counts) for the solution.

Steps to use the Count functions:

1. Open Chapter7.MathematicalFunctions.xlsx. Work on the *Counts* sheet.
2. Navigate to cell B12 and type the formula for COUNT.

```
= COUNT(A2:A10)
```

3. Navigate to cell B13 and type the formula for COUNTA.

```
= COUNTA(A2:A10)
```

4. Navigate to cell B14 and type the formula for COUNTIF.

```
= COUNTIF(A2:A10,">20")
```

Values	
10	
20	
1/1/2001	
40	
50	
1	
#DiV	
A	
Count	6
CountA	8
CountIF	3

Figure 7.1: Result of the Count functions.

In the above result, the COUNT function computed as a result of 6, as it counted the non-blank values, numbers, and the number represented as text (1).

The COUNTA function displayed a result of 8, as it has counted the error cell(#Div) and the text value (A) along with other non-blank values.

The COUNTIF function showed a result of 3 for the condition >20, as it considered the serial number of the date along with the values 40 and 50.

The SUM functions

Excel provides various of SUM functions such as SUM, SUMIF, and SUMIFS.

SUM function

The SUM function adds the values in the cells. It can sum individual values, cell references, or ranges.

Syntax:

=COUNT(value1, value2..)

SUMIF function

The SUMIF function is used to add the values in a range that meet specific criteria.

Syntax:

SUMIF(range, criteria, sum_range)

Where:

Range is the range of cells on which the criteria will be applied. *Criteria* is the condition which can be a number, expression, cell reference, text, or a function. *Sum_range* is optional and specifies the actual cells to be added. If omitted, Excel adds the cells that are specified in the range.

SUMIFS function

The SUMIFS function adds the values in the cells meeting multiple criteria.

Syntax:

SUMIFS(sum_range, criteria_range1, criteria1, criteria_range2, criteria2,…)

Exercise2: Use the enclosed Chapter7.MathematicalFunctions.xlsx (Sheet Orders) to perform this exercise.

- Calculate Total Sales by adding all the Sales values.
- Calculate the Total Sales for the Region = West.
- Calculate the Sales where Segment is Corporate and the Region is West.

Refer to Chapter7.MathematicalFunctions_Solutions.xlsx (Sheet Orders) for the solution.

Steps to use the SUM, SUMIF, and SUMIFS functions:

1. Open Chapter7.MathematicaFunctions.xlsx. Work on the *Orders* sheet.
2. To Calculate SUM.
   - Navigate to cell J21. Type the formula as =*SUM*
   - Insert an open parenthesis and select the range of cells in Column J (J2:J19) and close the parenthesis.
   - Press *Enter*.

   ```
   = SUM(J2:J19)
   ```

   This formula will display the sum of all the cells in column J.
3. Calculating Total Sales for the Region = West.
   The function SUMIF will be used since this calculation requires a condition.
   - Navigate to cell J22. Type =SUMIF, and then press *tab* on the keyboard.
   - Select the range of cells in column H (Region),
   - Provide the criteria for Region West and select the range of cells where Sum needs to be applied, i.e., column J.
   - The completed formula should appear as:

   ```
   =SUMIF(H2:H19,"West",J2:J19)
   ```

4. Calculating the Sales where Segment = Corporate and Region = West.
   The function SUMIFS will be used since this calculation requires checking for multiple conditions.
   - Navigate to cell J23. Type =SUMIFS and select the respective ranges to formulate a calculation as:

   ```
   =SUMIFS(J2:J19,G2:G19,"Corporate",H2:H19,"West")
   ```

In the above calculation, J2:J19 is the range of *Sales* column which needs to be added. G2:G19 is the range of the *Segment* column, and H2:H19 is the range for the *Region* column.

The results of the three calculations are shown below:

Total Sales	$	5,709.68
Total Sales of Region West	$	1,666.75
Sales for Segment Corporate and Region West	$	591.71

Figure 7.2: Result of the Sum functions.

Excel provides a wide range of functions, and these are some of the most commonly used Mathematical functions in Excel. To use these functions, simply enter the function name in a cell and provide the appropriate cell references or values within parentheses. Press Enter to execute a function, and Excel will perform the calculation and display the result in the cell.

Chapter 8
Lookup and Reference

The previous chapter explained Mathematical functions and their applications in performing calculations. This chapter will explore Lookup and reference functions, such as VLOOKUP, LOOKUP, INDEX, and MATCH. These Excel functions allow users to search for specific values, retrieve data from different parts of a worksheet, and perform lookups based on specific criteria.

The following topics will be discussed in this chapter:

- The VLOOKUP function
- The LOOKUP function
- The INDEX function
- The MATCH function

The VLOOKUP and LOOKUP are reference functions used to reference data stored in the same or different sheets/workbooks.

The VLOOKUP function

The VLOOKUP, also called vertical lookup is used to find related data in a table or a range. When VLOOKUP is used, Excel looks for the lookup value and then returns the corresponding data from a table or range in the same sheet or different sheet/workbook.

Syntax:
=VLOOKUP(lookup_value, table_array, col_index, range_lookup)

Where:

lookup_value: is the value to look up. This value must be in the first column of the range of cells specified in the table_array. It can be a value or a cell reference.

table_array: The range of cells in which the lookup_value is searched. It will return the corresponding data based on the lookup_value. The first column in the cell range must contain the lookup_value.

col_index: The column number (with value 1 for the left-most column of the table_array) that contains the return value.

range_lookup: This is an optional value that specifies if the return value should be an exact match or approximate. It is a logical value:

- Approximate match (1/True). It assumes that the first column in the range is sorted and will return the closest matched value. VLOOKUP uses approximate match by default if range_lookup is not specified.
- Exact match(0/False). This searches for the exact match in the first column.

How it works

The VLOOKUP function works by searching for the "Value to look up" in the first column of the specified range "where this value is located."

Once it finds a match, it returns the value from the specified "column number" in that range.

The "return an Approximate or Exact match" is indicated as 1/TRUE for an approximate match or 0/FALSE for an exact match.

VLOOKUP features

- It is useful in situations where one table/range contains an ID, and another table/range contains the corresponding ID/description. VLOOKUP can reference both tables, match the IDs, and return the corresponding descriptions.

- VLOOKUP searches for values to the right of the lookup value. It looks for the lookup value in the first column of the table/range and then searches to the right. It cannot search to the left of the lookup value.
- If the range_lookup parameter (true/false) is TRUE or not provided, the first column in the table/range needs to be sorted alphabetically or numerically.
  If the first column is not sorted, it may return unexpected values. To ensure an exact match, either sort the first column or use FALSE as the range_lookup parameter.

Look up value in the same sheet

The below exercise will demonstrate VLOOKUP when the lookup value is located in the same sheet.

Exercise1: Use the enclosed Chapter8.LookupAndReference.xlsx (Sheet Vlookup_SameSheet) to perform this exercise.

This workbook contains similar data as used in the previous chapters. In this sheet the Customer Name column is blank. The objective is to:

- Use VLOOKUP to retrieve Customer Names based on Customer IDs (Column F). Customer IDs and Names are located in the range F14 to G25.
- Use VLOOKUP to retrieve Product Names based on Product IDs (Column J). Product IDs and Names are located in the range J14 to M25.

*Refer to Chapter8.*LookupAndReference*_Solutions.xlsx (Sheet Vlookup_SameSheet) for the solution.*

Steps to use VLOOKUP when lookup value is located in the same sheet:

1. Open Chapter8.LookupAndReference.xlsx.
2. To get Customer Name.

a. Navigate to cell G2.
b. Type = VLOOKUP and press the tab key on the keyboard.
c. Select Cell F2 (Customer ID) to provide the lookup value,
d. Select the range F14:G25 to provide the table array (where Lookup value and description is located)
e. Type 2 to provide the col index. It is 2 because the range F14 to G25 contains only 2 columns, the first one being the lookup value.
f. Close the parenthesis and press *Enter*.
The VLOOKUP formula should appear like:

```
= VLOOKUP(F2,F14:G25,2)
```

This will produce incorrect results as the *Customer ID* column in the table_array (F14:G25) is not sorted and no value (true/false) is provided for the range_lookup.

To get the correct value, we need to either sort the *Customer ID* column in the table_array or provide *FALSE* in the range_lookup to get the exact match.

Modify the VLOOKUP formula to provide FALSE.

```
=VLOOKUP(F2,F14:G25,2,FALSE)
```

This will display the correct results.

3. If the value in G2 is correct, autofill the rest of the cells to fill the formula for the remaining cells in column G. This will apply the VLOOKUP formula to all the customer IDs in column F and automatically retrieve the corresponding customer names in column G.

Customer ID	Customer Name
JL-15175	James Lanier
DH-13675	Duane Huffman
AP-10915	Arthur Prichep
DM-12955	Dario Medina
HH-15010	Hilary Holden
CK-12205	Chloris Kastensmidt
BD-11620	Brian DeCherney
MH-17785	Maya Herman
PS-18970	Paul Stevenson
TG-21640	Trudy Glocke
VM-21835	Vivian Mathis

Figure 8.1: Finding Customer Name using VLookup.

4. To get Product Name.
   a. Navigate to Column K (Cell K2). Write the VLOOKUP formula as:

```
=VLOOKUP(J2,J14:P25,4,FALSE)
```

   In the above formula, note that col_index is specified as 4, which is the column number where the Product Name(located at M14) is found (starting from Product ID as the first column.)
5. If the value in cell K2 is correct, autofill the formula to the rest of the cells in Column K. This will populate the Product Names for all corresponding Product IDs.

Product ID	Product Name
TEC-PH-908	Panasonic Corded phone
FUR-BO-330	Sauder Bookcase
TEC-PH-909	Advantus Round Head Tacks
FUR-BO-331	Eureka Sanitaire Commercial
TEC-PH-910	Xerox 1986
FUR-BO-332	KI Conference Tables
TEC-PH-911	Eldon 200 Class Desk Accessories
FUR-BO-333	Avery Fluorescent Highlighters
TEC-PH-912	Office Star - Swivel Chair
FUR-BO-334	Metal Folding Chairs
TEC-PH-913	Innergie Charging Kit

Figure 8.2: Finding Product Name using VLookup.

Look up value in different sheets

In some scenarios, the lookup value may be located in different sheets. VLOOKUP is particularly useful in referencing data from other sheets.

The following exercise will demonstrate how to use VLOOKUP when the lookup value is located in different sheets.

Exercise2: Use the enclosed Chapter8.LookupAndReference.xlsx (Sheet Vlookup_DifferentSheets) to perform this exercise.

- Based on Customer IDs (Column F), retrieve the corresponding Customer Names. The Customer IDs and Names are located in a different sheet called "Customers".
- Based on the Product IDs (Column J), obtain the respective Product Names. The Product IDs and Names are located in a different sheet called "Products".

*Refer to Chapter8.*LookupAndReference*_Solutions.xlsx (Sheet Vlookup_DifferentSheets) for the solution.*

Steps to use VLOOKUP when the lookup value is located in different sheets:

1. Use the same workbook as used in the previous exercise and navigate to the sheet V_Lookup_DifferentSheets.
2. To get the Customer Name.
   - Navigate to cell G2.
   - Type = *VLOOKUP* and press the *Tab* key on the keyboard.
   - Select Cell F2 (Customer ID) to provide the lookup value and type ","
   - Then navigate to *Customers* sheet and select the range for *Customer ID* and *Customer Name* i.e., columns A1 to B12. The formula for VLOOKUP will be displayed on the formula bar at the top.
   - In the VLOOKUP on formula bar, type 2 as the col_index, type "," and *False* to get the exact match.
   - Close the parenthesis and press *Enter* on the keyboard.

   This will navigate you to the V_Lookup_DifferentSheets, and first Customer Name will be displayed.

   The VLOOKUP formula will appear like:

   ```
   =VLOOKUP(F2,Customers!A1:B12,2,FALSE)
   ```

   Observe that the range is displayed with the sheet name *Customers ! A1: B12*
3. If the value in G2 is correct, autofill the rest of the cells in Column G. Excel will automatically apply the VLOOKUP formula to the subsequent cells, adjusting the cell references accordingly, and display the corresponding Customer Names for each Customer ID.

Customer ID	Customer Name
JL-15175	James Lanier
DH-13675	Duane Huffman
AP-10915	Arthur Prichep
DM-12955	Dario Medina
HH-15010	Hilary Holden
CK-12205	Chloris Kastensm
BD-11620	Brian DeCherney
MH-17785	Maya Herman
PS-18970	Paul Stevenson
TG-21640	Trudy Glocke
VM-21835	Vivian Mathis

Figure 8.3: Customer Names displayed from a different sheet.

4. To get Product Name.
   - Navigate to cell K2.
   - Type = *VLOOKUP* and press the *Tab* key on the keyboard.
   - Select Cell J2 (Customer ID) to provide the lookup value and type ",".
   - Navigate to *Products* sheet and select the range for *Product ID* and *Product Name* i.e., columns A1 to D12. The formula for VLOOKUP will be displayed on the formula bar at the top.
   - In the VLOOKUP on formula bar, type 4 as the col_index. Type "," and *FALSE* to get the exact match.
   - Close the parenthesis and press *Enter* on the keyboard.

   This will navigate you to the V_Lookup_DifferentSheets, and the first Product Name will be displayed.

   The VLOOKUP formula will appear like:

   ```
   =VLOOKUP(J2,Products!A1:D12,4,FALSE)
   ```

   Observe that the range is displayed with the sheet name *Products ! A1: D12.*
5. If the value in K2 is correct, autofill the rest of the cells in column K.

Product ID	Product Name
TEC-PH-908	Panasonic Corded phone
FUR-BO-330	Sauder Bookcase
TEC-PH-909	Advantus Round Head Tacks
FUR-BO-331	Eureka Sanitaire Commercial
TEC-PH-910	Xerox 1986
FUR-BO-332	KI Conference Tables
TEC-PH-911	Eldon 200 Class Desk Accessories
FUR-BO-333	Avery Fluorescent Highlighters
TEC-PH-912	Office Star - Swivel Chair
FUR-BO-334	Metal Folding Chairs
TEC-PH-913	Innergie Charging Kit

Figure 8.4: Product Names displayed from a different sheet.

Look up value in different workbooks

In some scenarios, the lookup value may be located in different Excel workbooks. VLOOKUP is useful in referencing the data from different workbooks.

The exercise below will demonstrate how to use VLOOKUP when the lookup value is in a different workbook.

Exercise3: Use the enclosed Chapter8.LookupAndReference.xlsx (Sheet Vlookup_DifferentWorkbook) to perform this exercise.

- To get Customer Names based on Customer IDs (Column F), the data is located in a different Excel workbook called Customers.
- To get Product Names based on Product IDs (Column J), the data is located in a different Excel workbook called Products.

Refer to Chapter8.LookupAndReference_Solutions.xlsx (Sheet Vlookup_DifferentSheets) for the solution.

Steps to use VLOOKUP when the lookup value is located in different workbooks:

1. From the enclosed data set, open *Chapter8.Customers* and *Chapter8.Products* on your system. We will be taking Customer Name and Product Name from these workbooks.
2. Now, open Chapter8.LookupAndReference.xlsx. Navigate to the sheet V_Lookup_DifferentWorkbook.
3. To get Customer Name.
   - Navigate to cell G2.
   - Type = *VLOOKUP* and press the T*ab* key on the keyboard.
   - Select Cell F2 (Customer ID) to provide the lookup value and type ",".
   - Navigate to the Excel workbook *Customers.xlsx* and select the range for *Customer ID* and *Customer Name,* i.e., columns A1 to B12. The formula for VLOOKUP will be displayed on the formula bar at the top.
   - In the VLOOKUP on formula bar, type 2 as the col_index, then Type ",", and *FALSE* to get the exact match.
   - Close the parenthesis and press *Enter* on the keyboard. This will navigate you to the V_Lookup_DifferentWorkbook sheet, and the first Customer Name will be displayed.

   The VLOOKUP formula will appear like:

   ```
   =VLOOKUP(F2,[Chapter8.Customers.xlsx]Sheet1!$A$1:$B$12,2
   ,FALSE)
   ```

   Observe that the range is displayed with the workbook name [Chapter8.Customers.xlsx]Sheet1!$A$1:$B$12, and Excel automatically uses the absolute references for the columns in the range.
4. If the value in G2 is correct, autofill the rest of the cells in Column G.
5. To get Product Name.
   - Navigate to cell K2 in Chapter8.LookupAndReference.xlsx.
   - Type = *VLOOKUP* and press the T*ab* key on the keyboard.

- Select Cell J1 (Product ID) to provide the lookup value and type ",".
- Navigate to the Excel workbook *Products* and select the range for *Product ID* and *Product Name,* i.e., columns A1 to D12.
  The formula for VLOOKUP will be displayed on the formula bar at the top.
- In the VLOOKUP on formula bar, type 4 as the col_index. Type ",", and *FALSE* to get the exact match.
- Close the parenthesis and press *Enter* on the keyboard. This will navigate you to the V_Lookup_DifferentWorkbook sheet, and first Product Name will be displayed.

  The VLOOKUP formula will appear like:

  ```
  =VLOOKUP(F2,[Chapter8.Customers.xlsx]Sheet1!$A$1:$B$12,2
  ,FALSE)
  ```

  Observe that the range is displayed with the workbook name [Chapter8.Customers.xlsx]Sheet1!$A$1:$B$12, and Excel automatically uses the absolute references for the columns in the range.

6. If the value in K2 is correct, autofill the rest of the cells in Column K. The Customer Name and Product Name values will be the same as displayed in the previous exercises.

The LOOKUP function

The LOOKUP function, helps in searching for a value in a single row or column and finding the corresponding value from the same position in another single row or column.

Syntax: =
=LOOKUP(lookup_value, lookup_vector, [result_vector])

Where:

lookup_value: is the value that needs to be looked up.

lookup_vector: The one-row or one-column range to search.

result_vector: The one-row or one-column range of results.

VLOOKUP vs LOOKUP

Both functions are used for looking up the values, but VLOOKUP is more suited when the search is made across multiple rows and within specific columns. VLOOKUP searches on the right, the lookup column needs to be the first column in the range. On the other hand, whereas LOOKUP (in Microsoft 365 XLOOKUP) can look up values in any direction, allowing for more flexibility in searching.

Exercise4: Use the enclosed Chapter8.LookupAndReference.xlsx (Sheet Lookup) to perform this exercise.

This sheet contains columns such as, Name, ID, Revenue, Age, and Phone.

- Find the Revenue of ID 14872.
- Find the Age of ID 23948.
- Find the Name of ID 14872.
- Find the Phone number of ID 27361.

Refer to Chapter8.LookupAndReference_Solutions.xlsx (Sheet Lookup) for the solution.

Steps to use the LOOKUP function:

1. Continue using the same workbook used in the previous exercise. Navigate to the sheet *Lookup*.
2. Revenue of ID 14872
   - Navigate to cell B8.
   - Write the LOOKUP function as below:

```
=LOOKUP(B2,B2:B6,C2:C6)
```

Where lookup value is B2, B2:B6 is a range where the lookup value is located, and C2:C6 is the range where the lookup_vector or the searched value is located.

3. Age of ID 23948
   - Navigate to cell B9.
   - Write the LOOKUP function as below:

   ```
   =LOOKUP(B3,B2:B6,D2:D6)
   ```

4. Name of ID 14872
   - Navigate to cell B10.
   - Write the LOOKUP formula as below:

   ```
   =LOOKUP(B2,B2:B6,A2:A6)
   ```

   Observe in this formula, LOOKUP is looking to the left of the lookup value, which is not possible using VLOOKUP.

5. Phone number of ID 27361
   - Navigate to cell B11.
   - Write the LOOKUP formula as below:

   ```
   =LOOKUP(B4,B2:B6,E2:E6)
   ```

The result of the above LOOKUP functions is shown below:

Revenue of ID 14872	65000
Age of ID 23948	29
Name of ID 14872	Smith
Phone number of ID 27361	404-728-9217

Figure 8.5: Result of the LOOKUP function.

The INDEX function

The INDEX function is another useful reference/lookup function that returns the value of a cell in a specified range. INDEX can be used to retrieve individual values or entire rows and columns.

It is particularly valuable when dealing with large datasets as it allows easy retrieval of specific cell values (intersection of row and column). The INDEX function becomes even more beneficial when used in combination with other functions such as MATCH.

Syntax: =
INDEX(array, row_num, column_num)

Where:

array: refers to cell range. If range includes only one row or column, the corresponding row_num or column_num is optional.

row_num: The position of the row in the array/range.

column_num: It is optional and represents the column position in the array.

Exercise5: Use the enclosed Chapter8.LookupAndReference.xlsx (Sheet IndexMatch) to perform this exercise.

In this exercise, we will explore different ways to write the INDEX function, such as using the entire data as the range, using a specific column as a range, and using a specific row as the range.

- Use the entire data as the range and write an INDEX function to return the value of DM-12955 that is stored in F5.
- Use Column F as the range and write an INDEX function to return the value of DM-12955 that is stored in F5.
- Use row 5 as the range and write an INDEX function to return the value of DM-12955 that is stored in F5.

Refer to Chapter8.LookupAndReference_Solutions.xlsx (Sheet IndexMatch) for the solution.

Steps to use the INDEX function:

1. Return the value located at the intersection of row/column:
   - Navigate to cell F14 (or any cell of your choice) and write the formula using the INDEX function

   ```
   =INDEX(A1:O12,5,6)
   ```

   In the above formula A1:O12 is the range, number 5 is the row number, and 6 is the column number. This formula will return *DM-12955.*
2. Return the value when only one column (F) is selected as a range.
   - Navigate to cell F15 (or any cell of your choice) and write the formula using the INDEX function:

   ```
   =INDEX(F1:F12,5)
   ```

   In the above formula F1:F12 is the range of the Column F. Since only one column is selected, only the row number 5 is specified, and the column number is omitted. This formula will return *DM-12955.*
3. Return the value when only one row (5) is selected as a range.
   - Navigate to cell F16 (or any cell of your choice) and write the formula using the INDEX function

   ```
   =INDEX(A5:O5,6)
   ```

   In the above formula A5:O5 is the range of the row 5. Since, only one row is selected, only column number 6 is specified, and row number is omitted. This formula will return *DM-12955.*

Index when value is located at the intersection of row/column	DM-12955
Index when one column selected as range	DM-12955
Index when one row is selected as range	DM-12955

Figure 8.6: Result of the INDEX function.

Due to its ability to work with entire ranges, individual columns, or rows, the INDEX function provides users with flexible options for data lookup and reference.

The MATCH function

The MATCH function looks ups a specified value in a range of cells and returns the relative position of the value in the range.

Syntax:
= MATCH(lookup_value, lookup_array, match_type)

Where:

lookup_value: is the value that needs to be searched in the lookup_array /range.

Lookup_array: is the range of cells being searched.

match_type: This is optional and has a value of -1,0,or 1.

- If Omitted or set to 1. It returns the largest value that is less than or equal to the lookup_value. The values in the lookup_array must be in *ascending* order.
- If set to 0. It returns the exact match of the lookup_value.

- If set to -1. It returns the smallest value that is greater than or equal to the lookup_value. The lookup_array must be in *descending* order.

Exercise6: Use the enclosed Chapter8.LookupAndReference.xlsx (Sheet IndexMatch) to perform this exercise.

- Find the position of the Customer - Brian DeCherney

Refer to Chapter8.LookupAndReference_Solutions.xlsx (Sheet IndexMatch) for the solution.

Steps to use the MATCH function:

1. Search for Customer Name – Brian DeCherney and return its cell position.
   - Navigate to cell I14 (or any cell of your choice) and write the formula using the MATCH function

     ```
     =MATCH(G8,G2:G12,0)
     ```

     In the above formula, G8 is the lookup value (Brian DeCherney). G2:G12 is the range that contains this lookup value. 0 is the match type, which means an exact match should be used.

     The result of the above expression is 7. This indicates that Brian DeCherney is located at the 7th position in the range G2:G12.

Combining INDEX and MATCH function

Quite often, INDEX and MATCH functions are used together to perform dynamic lookups.

Exercise7: Use the enclosed Chapter8.LookupAndReference.xlsx (Sheet IndexMatch) to perform this exercise.

- Find the Sales of Customer - James Lanier.

In this exercise, we will first find the Sales using the INDEX function, and then use both INDEX and MATCH functions together to find the Sales. The output of both will be the same.
Refer to Chapter8.LookupAndReference_Solutions.xlsx (Sheet IndexMatch) for the solution.

Steps to use INDEX and MATCH to perform lookups:

1. Find the Sales using the INDEX function.
   - Navigate to cell L14 and write the formula using the INDEX function:

     ```
     =INDEX(G1:L12,2,6)
     ```

   This will return the Sales of 475.944 for Customer - James Lanier.

2. Use the MATCH function to find the position of the Sales
   - Navigate to cell L15 and write the formula using the MATCH function:

     ```
     =MATCH(L2,L1:L12,0)
     ```

   This will return the position of Sales 475.944 i.e., 2.

3. Combining the INDEX and MATCH function in one calculation.
   - Navigate to cell L16 and write the formula as below:

     ```
     =INDEX(G1:L12,MATCH(L2,L1:L12,0),6)
     ```

The above calculation replaces the row_num of the INDEX function with the position returned by MATCH function and obtains the same result.

Find Sales using Index	475.944
Find the position using Match	2
Index+Match	475.944

Figure 8.7: Result of combining INDEX and MATCH functions.

Chapter 9
Pivot tables and Charts

The previous chapter provided an explanation on Lookup and Reference functions and how they can be used in searching for a value in a dataset. This chapter will delve into summarizing data using Pivot tables and Charts. With pivot tables, users can quickly generate reports, perform calculations, and create visualizations without the need for complex formulas or manual data manipulation.

The following topics will be discussed in this chapter:

- Understanding Pivot tables
- Creating PivotTables
- Charts
- Updating PivotTable data

Understanding Pivot Tables

A Pivot table is created using a range of cells or a table. It serves as a valuable tool for calculating, summarizing, and analyzing data. It helps in understanding a large data set by drawing comparisons, identifying patterns and trends. By transforming data into rows and columns and perform calculations, it empowers users to generate insightful reports in Excel.

To create a successful Pivot table:

- All columns should have headers
- There should not be any blank cells or columns
- It should not have merged cells.

Pivot table is created by selecting *Insert* > *Pivot Table* from the ribbon.

Pivot Table Interface

The data contained in Chapter9.PivotTable (Sheet SourceData) is utilized to illustrate the Pivot table interface.

The steps to be followed to create a pivot table are:

1. Open Chapter9.PivotTable.xlsx. Navigate to the Sheet SourceData.
2. Navigate to the *Insert* in the ribbon, select *Pivot Table* and then choose *From Table/ Range*. In the subsequent *PivotTable from table or range* dialog box, select *New Worksheet*.

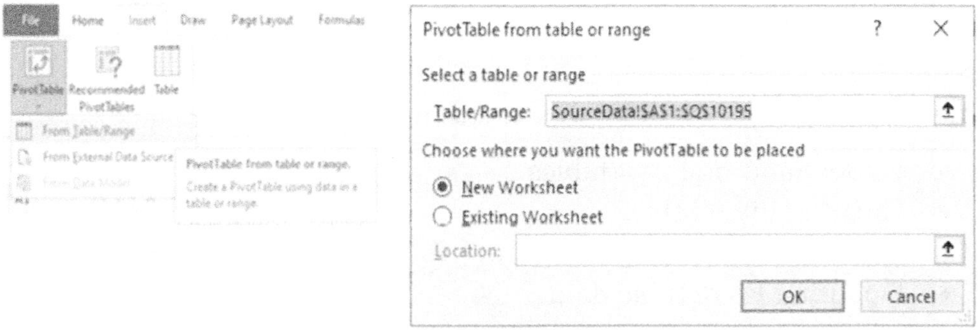

Figure 9.1: Option to create a Pivot table.

This will create a new sheet displaying the Pivot Table interface, with the view/report on the left and *PivotTable Fields* on the right.

3. Pivot table Interface has the format as shown below.

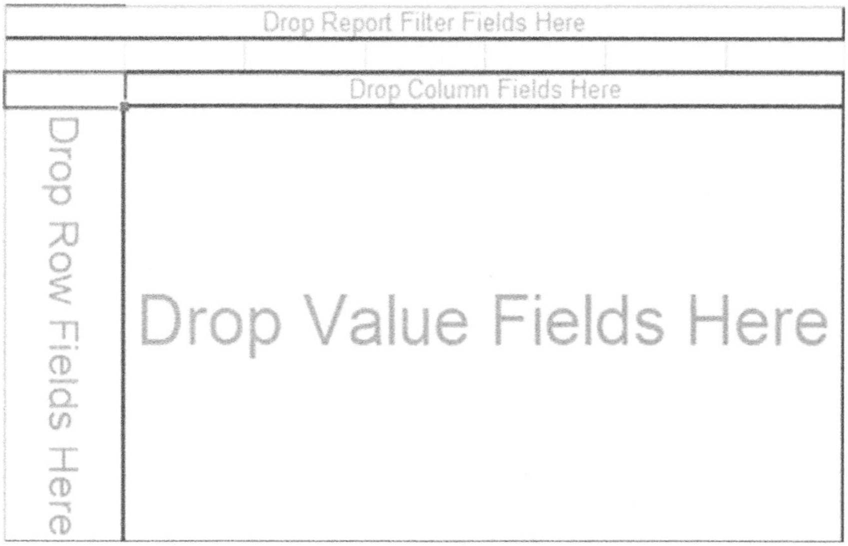

Figure 9.2: Pivot table Interface.

When fields are selected from the *PivotTable fields*, they are displayed here.

4. The Pivot Table Fields offer the following options:

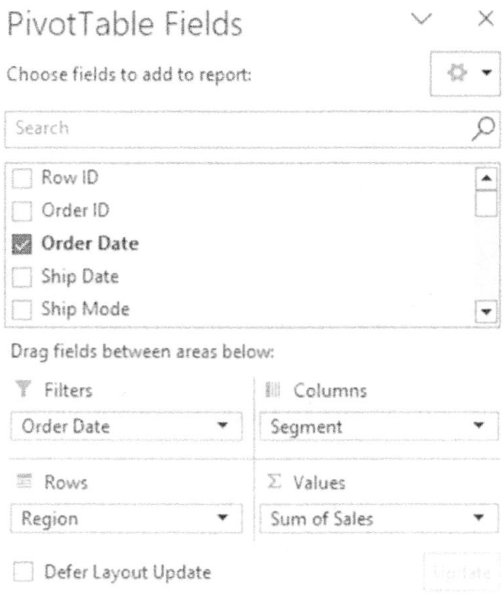

Figure 9.3: PivotTable Fields.

a. Choose fields to add to report.
   This section displays all the fields available in the selected data. As fields are selected, they will appear in the view. Fields can be dragged/dropped under *Filters, Columns, Rows* and *Values* as needed. To access field properties, click on the drop-down arrow next to the respective field.
b. Filters.
   The fields dropped here will serve as filters for the view/report.
c. Columns.
   The Pivot table displays data in a column and Row format. Drop the fields that want to be displayed in columns here.
d. Rows.
   Drop here the fields that are to be displayed in rows.
e. Values.
   Any numeric fields, such as Sales or Profit, on which aggregation needs to be performed, will be displayed here.

As the fields are selected, they will form the PivotTable view/report. Fields can be formatted to include a dollar sign, etc.

Order Date	(All)			
Sum of Sales	Segment			
Region	Consumer	Home Office	Corporate	Grand Total
South	$ 195,580.97	$ 74,255.00	$121,885.93	$ 391,721.91
West	$ 363,974.74	$143,491.11	$232,347.76	$ 739,813.61
East	$ 357,141.86	$131,109.68	$203,576.63	$ 691,828.17
Central	$ 253,962.22	$ 91,212.64	$157,995.81	$ 503,170.67
Grand Total	$1,170,659.79	$440,068.43	$715,806.13	$2,326,534.35

Figure 9.4: PivotTable created from the selection fields.

In the above PivotTable, *Order Date* is displayed as a filter, *Region* as Rows, *Segment* as Columns, and *Sales* as the aggregated value.

Please Rename this PivotTable sheet as *Pivot1*.

5. When a Pivot Table is selected, the ribbon displays two options - PivotTable Analyze and Design.

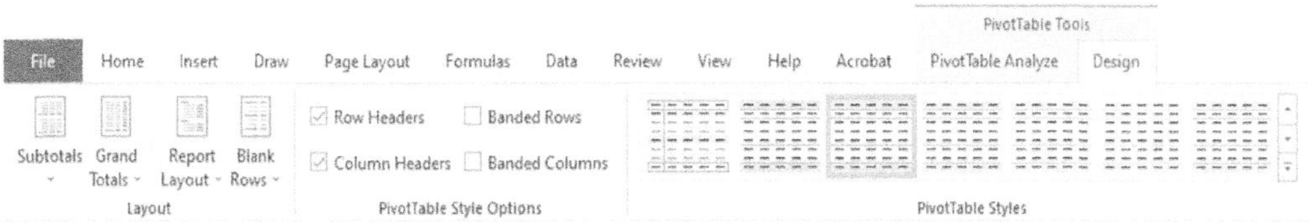

Figure 9.5: PivotTable Analyze and Design options.

   a. PivotTable Analyze. Use this option to add *Slicer* to the Pivot table. Additionally, find Calculations, Charts, and Recommended PivotTables options available here. If the underlying source data changes, refresh the Pivot table by selecting the *Refresh* option.
   b. Design. Use this option to control the layout, including Subtotals, Grand Totals, Report Layout, Blank Rows, as well as *PivotTable Style* options.

The formatting of a PivotTable can be done in the same fashion as with any other cell or sheet in Excel.

Creating Pivot table

A Pivot table is created to summarize data within a sheet in the workbook. The following exercise will explain how to create a Pivot table to draw meaningful results from the data.

Exercise1: Use the enclosed Chapter9.PivotTable (Sheet SourceData) to perform this exercise.

- Create a Pivot table to display Sales by Customers and count the number of Orders for each Customer.
- Use the Order Date to filter data by Years.
- Format Sales with a $ sign and show two decimal places.
- Display the Top 10 Customers by Sales.

Refer to Chapter9.PivotTable_Solutions.xlsx (Sheet PivotTable2) for the solution.

Steps to create PivotTable to find the Sales by Customers:

1. Open Chapter9.PivotTable.xlsx and navigate to the sheet *SourceData.*
2. From the ribbon, navigate to *Insert,* and from the *PivotTable* drop-down, select *From Table/Range.*
   Choose the default range and ensure to use the option *New WorkSheet*. This will display the PivotTable interface on a new sheet.
3. From the *PivotTable Fields*:
   a. Select the fields *Customer Name*, *Order ID*, *Order Date* and *Sales.* *Customer Name, Order Date* fields, and *Order ID* will be displayed under *Rows. Sales* will be displayed under *Values.*
      Excel automatically aggregates *Order Date* into different Date fields such as Years, Quarters, Months etc., and also displays Order Date.
      Click on the drop-down arrows next to Quarters, Months, and Order Date (one-by-one) and select *Remove Field*. Ensure that only *Years(Order Date)* is displayed.

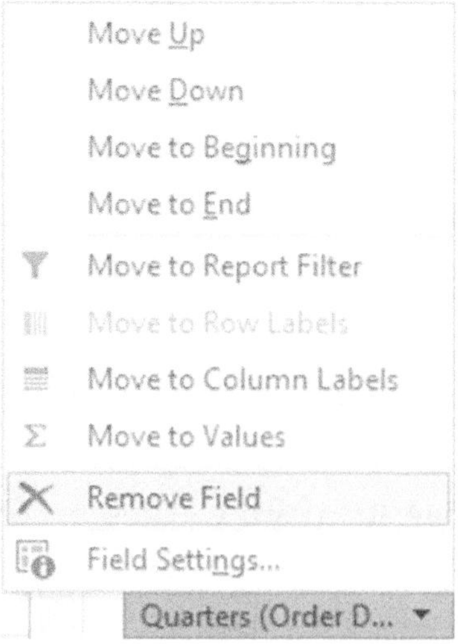

Figure 9.6: Removing the fields from the Rows.

   b. Drag *Years (Order Date)* from *Rows* to *Filters* section. This will create a filter on the Pivot table for Years.
4. Obtain Count of Order IDs.
   Currently, individual Order Ids are displayed on the Pivot Table. To create a count, drag *Order ID* from *Rows* to *Values* section.
   After making all the above changes, the PivotTable field selection will appear as shown below:

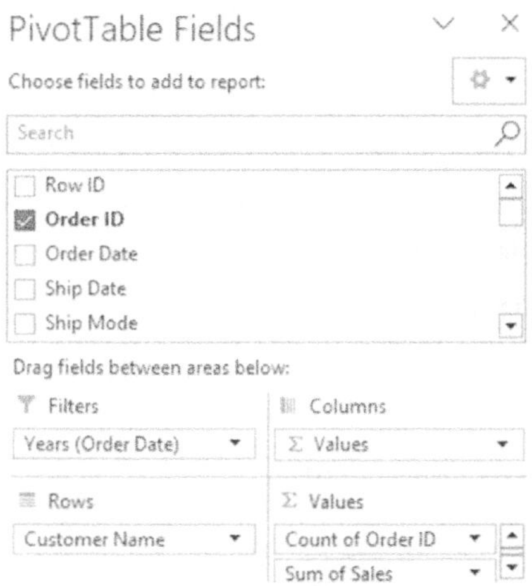

Figure 9.7: PivotTable field selections.

5. Display *Sales* with a $ sign and 2 decimal places.
   Highlight the *Sum of Sales* column on the PivotTable, and from the *Home* tab in the ribbon select "$".
6. Display the Top 10 Customers by Sales.
   a. On the Pivot Table, navigate to *Customer Name* and click the filter drop-down next to it.
   b. Select *Value Filters* and then choose *Top 10*.
   c. In the subsequent *Top 10 Filter* dialog *for Customer Name,* select *Sum of Sales* from the drop-down menu.

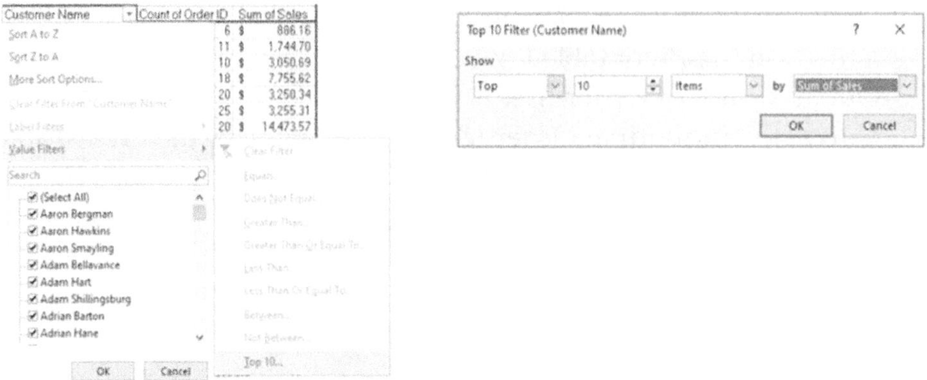

Figure 9.8: Filter displaying Top 10 Customers.

This will display only the Top 10 Customers in the Pivot Table. If the $ sign disappears from the Sales, add it again from the *Home* ribbon. The labels on the Pivot table can be renamed.

After applying the Top 10 filter, the resulting Pivot table will appear as shown below:

Years (Order Date)	(All)	
	Data	
Customer Name	**Count of Order ID**	**Sum of Sales**
Adrian Barton	20	$ 14,473.57
Christopher Conant	11	$ 12,129.07
Hunter Lopez	11	$ 12,873.30
Ken Lonsdale	29	$ 14,175.23
Raymond Buch	18	$ 15,117.34
Sanjit Chand	22	$ 14,142.33
Sanjit Engle	19	$ 12,209.44
Sean Miller	15	$ 25,043.05
Tamara Chand	12	$ 19,052.22
Tom Ashbrook	10	$ 14,595.62
Grand Total	**167**	**$ 153,811.17**

Figure 9.9: Final output of the PivotTable.

d. Rename the Pivot table sheet as Pivot2.

The above PivotTable displays filter by Years(Order Date), Customer Name, Count of Order ID, and Sum of Sales. It also shows Top 10 Customers by Sales.

Exercise2: Use the enclosed Chapter9.PivotTable (Sheet SourceData) to perform this exercise.

- Create a Pivot table to display Sales by Category and Sub-Category. Display Subtotals and Grand Totals.
- Use the Order Date to place a filter for Years.
- Calculate the Percentage of Sales for each Category and Sub-Category.
- Display a calculated field to calculate Cost as Sales/Quantity.
- Filter the results by Year = 2019, and Category = Furniture.

Refer to Chapter9.PivotTable_Solutions.xlsx (Sheet PivotTable3) for the solution.

Steps to create a PivotTable to find the Sales by Category and SubCategory.

1. In the Chapter9.PivotTable.xlsx workbook, navigate to the sheet named *SourceData.*
2. From the ribbon, navigate to the *Insert* tab. Then, from the *PivotTable* drop-down, select *From Table/Range.*
   Choose the default range and make sure to use the option for *New WorkSheet*. This will display the PivotTable interface on a new sheet.
3. From the *PivotTable Fields*:
   - Select the fields *Order Date, Category, Sub-Category, and Sales.*
   - Except for the *Years (Order Date), r*emove all the other date fields. These fields can also be removed from the bottom of the field list.
   - Move *Years (Order Date)* from *Rows* to the *Filters* section.
     This will display *Years (Order Date), Category, Sub-Category,* and Total on the Pivot table. It also displays Sub-totals by Category.
   - With the PivotTable selected, navigate to *Design* option in the ribbon and explore the options for Subtotals and Grandtotals.

- If Subtotals are not displayed, select the option *Show all Subtotals at the bottom of Group.*

4. Calculate Percentage of Sales by Category and Sub-Category.
   - In the *PivotTable Fields*, drag *Sales* from the field list to the *Values* section. It will appear as *Sum of Sales2.*
   - Click on the drop-down arrow next to *Sum of Sales2* and select *Value Field Settings.* In the dialog box, click on the tab *Show Values As* and from the drop-down list under *Show Values as,* select *% of Parent Row Total.*

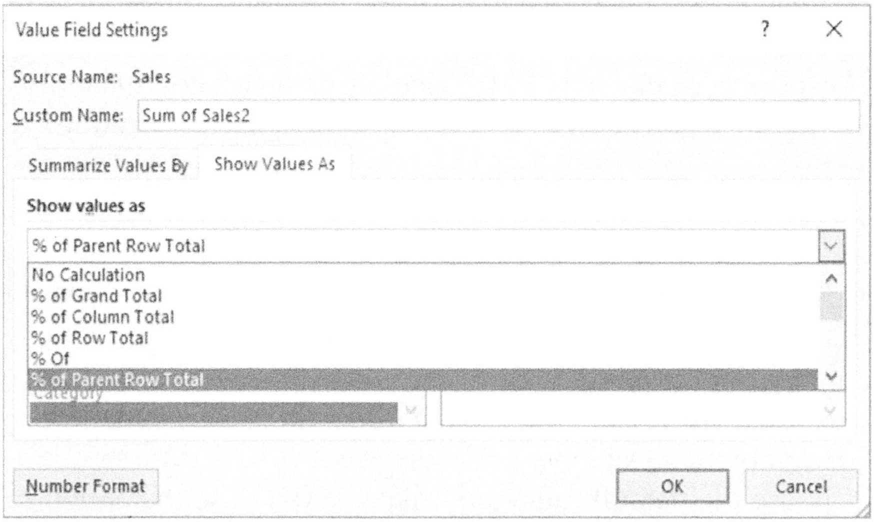

Figure 9.10: Calculating % of Total.

This will display a column Sum of Sales2 as a percentage on the PivotTable. Rename this column to % of Sales.

Note: The % of Sales for Sub-Category is calculated based on the Category Sub-Total, and Category level % of Sales will be calculated based on the Grand Total.

5. Create a calculated field to calculate Cost as Sales/Quantity.
   - From the *PivotTable Fields*, select *Quantity*. It will appear as *Sum of Quantity* under the *Values* section.

If *Quantity* is displayed in the PivotTable with a $ sign, remove the $ sign by formatting it as *General.*

- Navigate to *PivotTable Analyze* ribbon and select *Fields, Items, & Sets.* Then, choose *Calculated Field.*

  In the *Insert Calculated Field* dialog, name the field as *Cost* and create a formula by selecting the fields from the list.

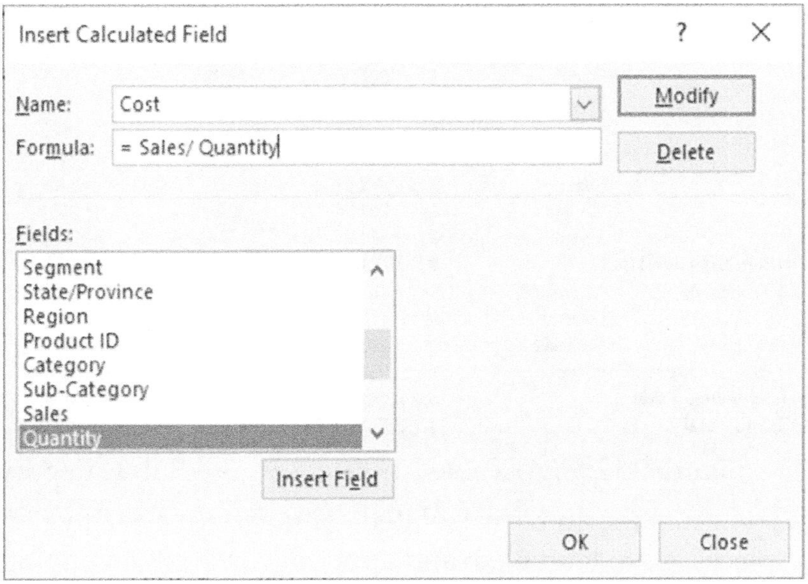

Figure 9.11: Calculated field for Cost.

This will display the calculated field as Sum of Cost on the Pivot table. After implementing all the above changes, the resulting Pivot table will appear as shown below:

Years (Order Date)	(All)				
		Data			
Category	Sub-Category	Sum of Sales	% of Sales	Sum of Quantity	Sum of Cost
⊟ Furniture	Bookcases	$ 115,361.20	15.28%	878	$ 131.39
	Chairs	$ 335,768.25	44.49%	2431	$ 138.12
	Furnishings	$ 95,598.13	12.67%	3799	$ 25.16
	Tables	$ 208,020.18	27.56%	1261	$ 164.96
Furniture Total		**$ 754,747.76**	**32.44%**	**8369**	**$ 90.18**
⊟ Office Supplies	Appliances	$ 108,213.19	14.79%	1750	$ 61.84
	Art	$ 27,659.01	3.78%	3092	$ 8.95
	Binders	$ 207,354.88	28.33%	6071	$ 34.15
	Envelopes	$ 16,528.36	2.26%	914	$ 18.08
	Fasteners	$ 8,532.24	1.17%	980	$ 8.71
	Labels	$ 12,695.04	1.73%	1410	$ 9.00
	Paper	$ 79,540.54	10.87%	5207	$ 15.28
	Storage	$ 224,644.55	30.69%	3191	$ 70.40
	Supplies	$ 46,725.50	6.38%	653	$ 71.56
Office Supplies Total		**$ 731,893.31**	**31.46%**	**23268**	**$ 31.45**
⊟ Technology	Accessories	$ 167,380.32	19.93%	2976	$ 56.24
	Copiers	$ 150,745.29	17.95%	242	$ 622.91
	Machines	$ 189,925.03	22.61%	442	$ 429.69
	Phones	$ 331,842.64	39.51%	3357	$ 98.85
Technology Total		**$ 839,893.28**	**36.10%**	**7017**	**$ 119.69**
Grand Total		**$2,326,534.35**	**100.00%**	**38654**	**$ 60.19**

Figure 9.12: PivotTable by Category and Sub-Category.

To format the above calculated column with a $ sign and 2 decimal places, go to Home tab and apply the desired formatting.

Charts in Excel

Charts in Excel are visual representations of data that make it easier to understand and analyze complex information. Excel offers a wide variety of chart types, such as bar charts, column charts, line charts, pie charts, scatter plots, and more, allowing users to choose the best-suited chart for their data.

Excel has two types of charts – Standard Charts and Pivot chart. Most of the functionalities are similar between the two charts except for few differences.

Standard Charts vs Pivot charts

1. Standard charts are created from the *Insert* tab, in the *Chart* group on the ribbon. Pivot Charts are created from the *Insert* tab, in the *Chart* group (PivotChart) on the ribbon. PivotCharts can also be created from *PivotTable Analyze* option, which is displayed once PivotTable is selected.
2. Standard charts are connected to the source data/ worksheet cells. Pivot Charts are based on the PivotTable data source (PivotTable fields).
3. Using Standard charts any kind of charts can be created. However, PivotCharts cannot create Scatter or Stock charts.

Standard Charts

Standard charts are created from the *Insert* tab, in the *Chart* group on the ribbon. These charts are connected to the source data/ worksheet cells.

To create a chart:

- Select the data or range to visualize, then click on the "Insert" tab in the Excel ribbon and navigate to the *Charts* group.
- Choose the desired chart type for Excel to automatically generate the chart based on the selected data.
- Excel also provides *Recommended Charts* option, based on the data present in the sheet.
- The chart can be customized to suit the requirements. Excel provides options to add titles, labels, data labels, legends, and even change the chart's colors and styles.

Excel's intuitive interface allows for quick chart creation and customization, enabling users to add titles, labels, and other elements to enhance the visual representation.

Exercise3: Use the enclosed Chapter9.PivotTable (Sheet SourceData) to perform this exercise.
Create a copy of the SourceData sheet and perform the following:

- Create a bar chart to display top 10 customers by sales.

Refer to Chapter9.PivotTable_Solutions.xlsx (Sheet Std_SourceData) for the solution.

Steps to create Standard bar Chart:

1. In the Chapter9.PivotTable.xlsx workbook, navigate to the sheet named *SourceData* and make a copy of the sheet. Name this sheet Std_SourceData.
2. Select the Sales column (Column N) and then go to the *Home* tab in the ribbon and navigate to *Sort & Filter* option in the *Editing* group.
3. Choose the option for *Sort Largest to Smallest,* and in the subsequent box, select *Expand this selection*. This will display top 10 customers by sales.
4. Now, select the column/ranges that will be used to create the chart. From the Customer Column (column G), select G1 thru G11. Press CTRL on the keyboard and select the corresponding Sales, i.e., cells N1 though N11.
5. Go to *Insert* tab on the ribbon and from the *Charts* group, either choose the *Recommended Charts,* or select the drop down next to the bar chart icon and choose the bar chart.

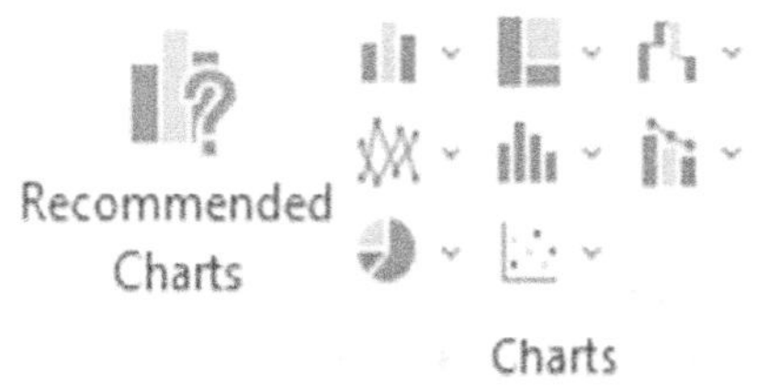

Figure 9.13: Selecting a chart to display.

6. This will create a bar chart, depicting the top 10 customers by Sales.

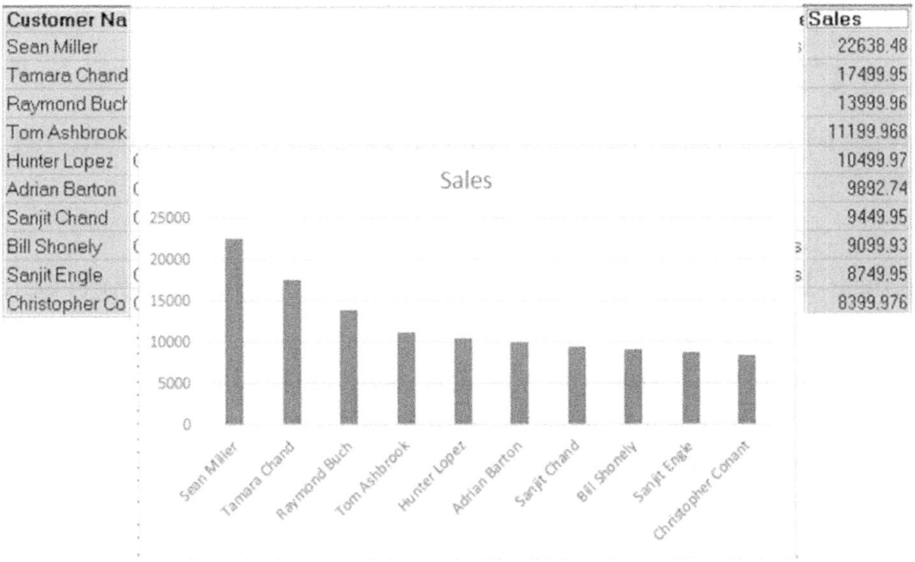

Figure 9.14: Bar chart based on the Customers and Sales selection.

7. When the chart is selected, it displays a *Chart Design* tab in the menu, which can be used to enhance the chart.

Figure 9.15: Chart design options.

A chart type can also be changed to display the data using a different chart.

Pivot Charts

To create a Pivot chart, we need to first create a Pivot table as they are based on the PivotTable data source.

Exercise4: Use the enclosed Chapter9.PivotTable (Sheet SourceData) to perform this exercise.

- Create a Pivot table to display Sales by various Regions.
- Use the Order Date to place a filter for Years.
- Create visualizations, such as bar charts, pie charts etc., to display this data.

  Refer to Chapter9.PivotTable_Solutions.xlsx (Sheet Charts) for the solution.

Steps to create a PivotTable and Charts.

1. In the Chapter9.PivotTable.xlsx workbook, navigate to the sheet named *SourceData.*
2. Creating Pivot table.
   - From the ribbon, go to the *Insert* tab, select *Pivot Table,* and choose the default range. Create a Pivot table on a new sheet.
   - In the *PivotTable Fields,* select *Order Date.* It will be displayed under the *Rows* section. Remove all the other date fields except Year (Order Date) and move it to *Filters.*
   - Select *Region* and *Sales. Region* will be displayed in the *Rows,* and *Sales* will be displayed in the *Values* section.
   - Select all values under *Sales* in the PivotTable and change the formatting to display a $ sign in front of the numbers.
     Rename this sheet as *RegionWise Sales.*
     The PivotTable will appear as shown below:

Years (Order Date)	(All)
Sum of Sales	
Region	Total
South	$ 391,721.91
West	$ 739,813.61
East	$ 691,828.17
Central	$ 503,170.67
Grand Total	**$2,326,534.35**

Figure 9.16: PivotTable for Region-wise Sales.

3. Creating PivotChart. PivotChart is connected to the data in the PivotTable.
   - Click anywhere on the PivotTable, go to the *PivotTable Analyze* tab in the ribbon. From the *Tools* group, select *PivotChart*.
   - By default, a chart will be selected (e.g., Clustered Column).

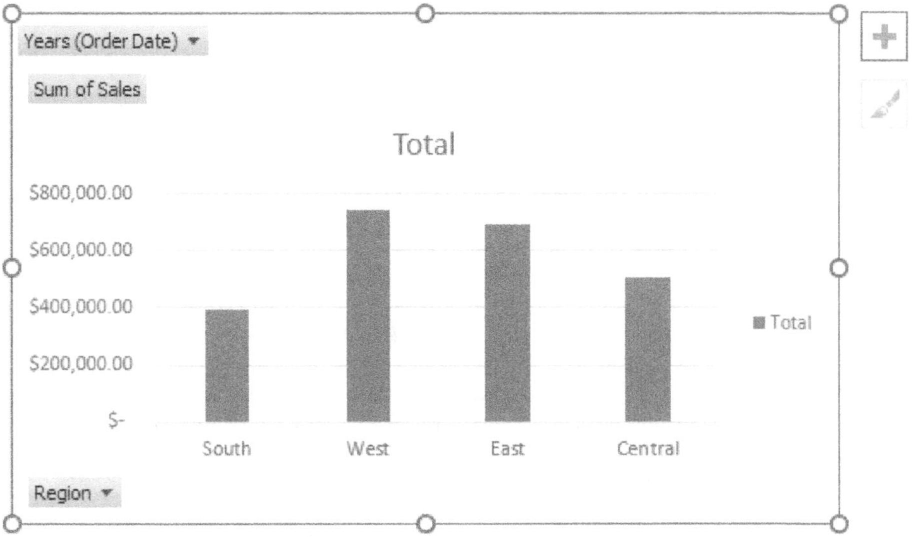

Figure 9.17: Clustered Column Chart.

The Chart displays Regions on the X-axis and Sum(Sales) on the Y-axis. It also includes filter for Years (Order Date) and Region. The blue (dot) Total on the right side shows the legend for the Region bar.

Select the plus (+) symbol on the right of the chart to explore various Chart Elements.

- Click on the text "Total" in between to enter the Chart title "Sales by Region".

4. Create a pie chart.

a. Select the PivotTable. From *PivotChart Analyze* option, choose *PivotChart,* and from the list of Charts, select *Pie.* This will display a pie chart with slices representing Sales in various Regions.

b. Displaying percentages on the pie chart.

Pie charts should display percentage of total instead of the whole amount.

i. In the chart, right-click on the pie slices and select *Add Data Labels.*

ii. Right-click on the slices again and select *Format Data Labels.*

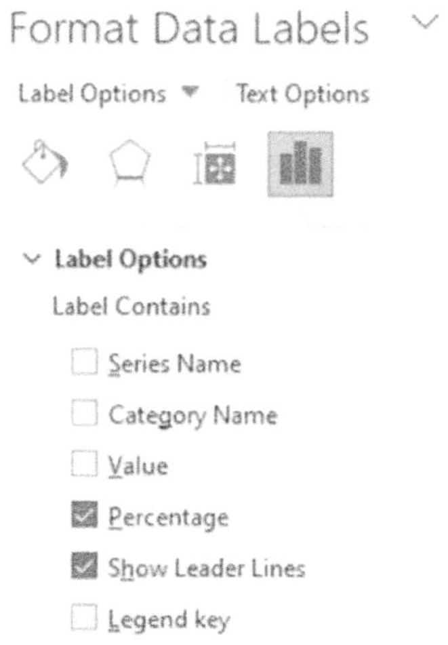

Figure 9.18: Displaying percentages on a pie chart.

This will display percentages on the pie slices. Change the title of the chart to "Sales % by Regions"
The resulting chart will appear as shown below:

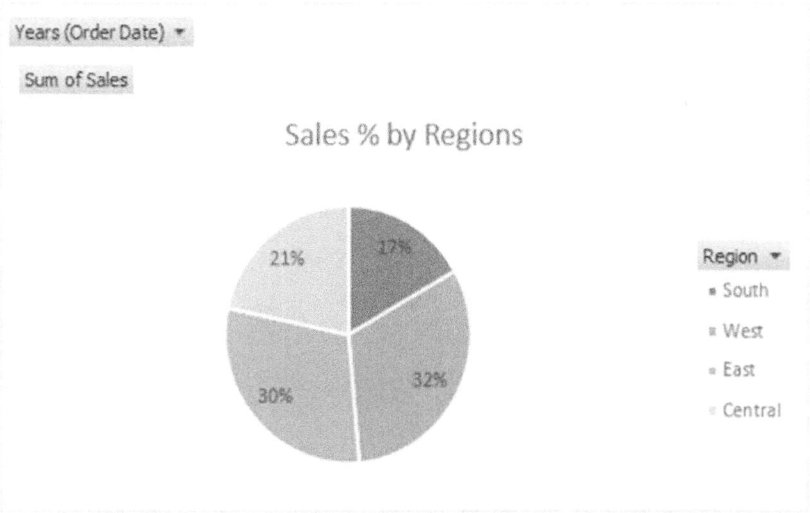

Figure 9.19: Pie chart displaying Sales percentages.

To change the chart type, right-click on the existing chart and select *Change Chart Type* to choose a different chart for data representation.

Updating PivotTable Data

The Pivot table needs to be refreshed whenever the underlying source data updates or changes. To refresh the data, select any cell within the PivotTable, and then choose the *Refresh* option from the *PivotTable Analyze* menu.

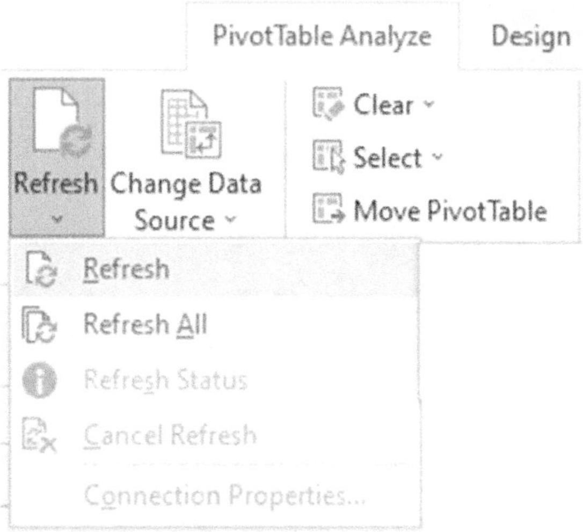

Figure 9.20: Refreshing the PivotTable.

Select *Refresh* to refresh data in the current PivotTable. If multiple PivotTables are present in the workbook select *Refresh All*.

Updating the PivotTable with New Data Rows

Since the PivotTable is based on a specific range, if a new row is added to the source data, the PivotTable range needs to be adjusted accordingly.

To update the range of the PivotTable:

- Select any cell on the PivotTable
- Navigate to *PivotTable Analyze* and select *Change Data Source*. When Change Data Source is selected, it will provide an option to change the existing range.

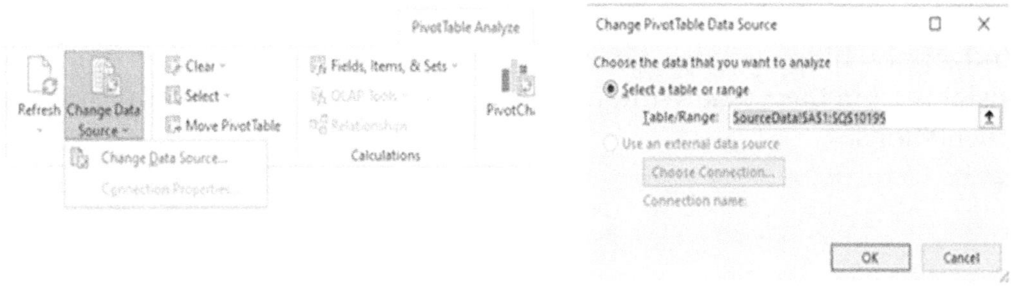

Figure 9.21: Updating PivotTable with new rows of data.

Automatically Updating the PivotTable on open

A PivotTable can also be automatically updated when the Workbook is opened. To enable this feature, select the PivotTable, navigate to the *PivotTable Analyze* tab in the menu, and click *Options* on the left. In the subsequent *PivotTable Options* dialog, go to the *Data* tab and check the *Refresh data when opening the file* option.

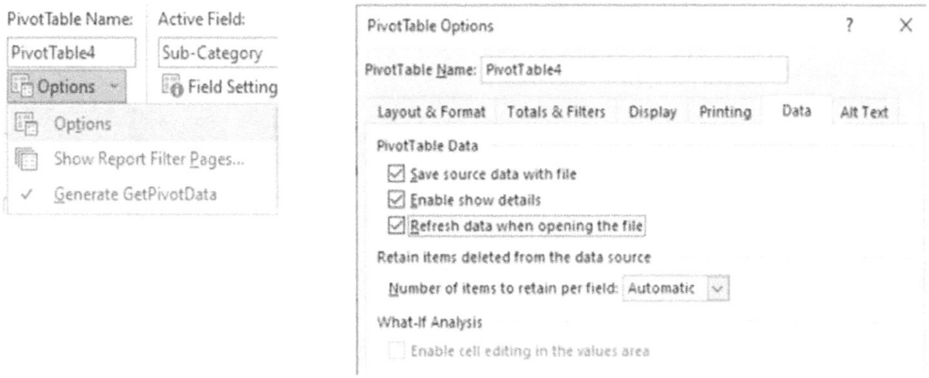

Figure 9.2: Updating the PivotTable on Open.

Excel PivotTables are a valuable tool for data analysis and reporting, offering an efficient and dynamic way to summarize large datasets. By allowing users to pivot and rearrange data, calculate various summaries, and apply filters easily, PivotTables empower users to gain valuable insights from their data without the need for complex formulas or manual calculations.

Chapter 10
Excel Table

The previous chapter provided an explanation on PivotTables and how they can be used summarizing and aggregating data in the worksheet. This chapter will explain the usage of Excel Tables. Excel tables provide additional functionality over the range of cells and provide an easy way of organizing, and standardization of data.

The following topics will be discussed in this chapter:

- Overview of Excel Tables
- Creating an Excel Table
- Subtotal

Overview of Excel Tables

Excel tables provide added functionality to a range of cells making them more dynamic. They help in easier organization, management and analyzing of related data. An Excel table can be created from the *Home* (Format as Table) or the *Insert* tab (table) in the ribbon. Any worksheet data can be converted to a Table.

Components of an Excel table:

An Excel table consists of the following components:

- Default Header row. By default, a table has a header row. Each header column displays a drop-down for filtering and sorting. When creating a table, users can specify if the data contains headers. If this option is not selected, Excel automatically creates a default header row.
- Visible header row. In a large dataset, the header row is always visible.

- Banded row. By default, all rows in the table are displayed with shading or banding to distinguish the rows of data.
- Table Design. When a cell inside a table is selected, the ribbon displays *Table Design.* It can be used to control the properties of the table by selecting/unselecting them.
- Total row. When the Total Row option is selected from Table Design, it adds a row with Totals. The cells on the total row display a drop-down to perform calculations such as Average, Count, Sum, etc. When one of these options is selected, Excel automatically converts them to a SUBTOTAL function, which ignores the filtered rows while performing the calculation.
- Automatic addition of Row/Column. To add a new row, navigate to the last cell and press the *Tab* key on the keyboard. To add a new column, simply start typing a column header next to the last column in the table, and a new column will be added automatically.
- Automatic Autofill. When a calculation is created in a cell of a column, it is automatically filled in all the cells of the column. Autofill is not required.
- Slicer option. To further filter the data, Excel Tables provide the option to add a Slicer from the *Insert* tab. Slicers allow users to visually filter data in the table.
- Resizing of Table. The last cell of the table displays a sizing handle that can be used to drag and increase the size of the table.
- Dynamic Pivot Table/Charts. When an Excel table is used as the source data for a Pivot Table/Chart, it refreshes dynamically when data updates or a new row is added, ensuring that the Pivot Table/Chart always reflects the most recent data.

Excel Tables provide added functionalities as compared to regular data in the range of cells.

Creating an Excel table

An Excel table is created from a range of cells. Data from any worksheet can be converted to an Excel table.

Exercise1: Use the enclosed Chapter10.ExcelTable (Sheet SourceData) to perform this exercise.

- Convert the Source Data to an Excel table.
- Add a new Calculation in Column 0 as New Sales = Sales * Discount

  Refer to Chapter10.ExcelTable_Solutions.xlsx (Sheet Table) for the solution.

Steps to create an Excel Table:

1. Open Chapter10_ExcelTable.xlsx and navigate to the sheet *SourceData.*
2. Make a copy of the *Source Data* sheet to preserve the original data for comparison.
   a. Right-click on the *Source Data* sheet and select *Move or Copy,* then choose *(move to end)* from the list. Select the option *Create a copy* at the bottom.
   b. Rename the new sheet as *Table.*
3. Create an Excel Table.
   a. Select any cell within the data range, then go to the *Insert* tab in the ribbon and click on *Table.* The Create Table dialog will appear with the range of the cells pre-selected. Make sure to check the option *My table has headers.*

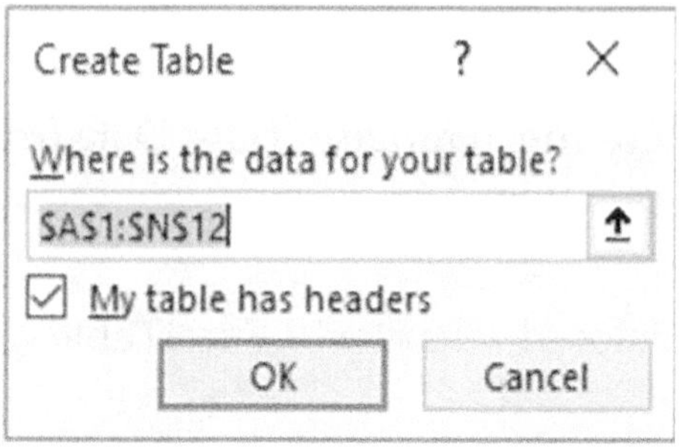

Figure 10.1: Create Table option.

This will create an Excel table with headers and banded rows.

Once the Table is created, it will display the *Table Design* option on the ribbon. On the extreme right, it shows the Table name. The default Table name can be changed here.

4. Add a calculation for New Sales.
   a. Navigate to cell O2. Type "=" and create the calculation by selecting K2, typing "*" and then selecting M2.
   b. Press Enter. The formula in the cell O2 will be auto-filled to all the cells in column O.
   c. Rename the Column as "New Sales".

The resulting Excel Table will appear as shown below:

Order Date	Ship Mode	Ship Date	Customer ID	Customer Name	Segment	Region	Product ID	Product Name	Sales	Quantity	Discount	Profit	New Sales
1/1/2021	Priority Delive	1/2/2021	JL-15175	James Lanier	Home Offic	West	TEC-PH-908	Panasonic Corded phone	$ 475.94	7	0.2	$ 59.49	$ 95.19
2/1/2021	Standard Freig	2/10/2021	DH-13675	Duane Huffman	Home Offic	West	FUR-BO-330	Sauder Bookcase	$ 411.33	4	0.15	$ (4.84)	$ 61.70
3/1/2021	Priority Delive	3/2/2021	AP-10915	Arthur Prichep	Consumer	South	TEC-PH-909	Advantus Round Head Tacks	$ 11.85	3	0	$ 3.79	$ -
4/1/2021	Second Class	4/7/2021	DM-12955	Dario Medina	Corporate	East	FUR-BO-331	Eureka Sanitaire Commercial	$ 795.41	6	0.2	$ 59.66	$ 159.08
5/1/2021	Priority Delive	5/2/2021	HH-15010	Hilary Holden	Corporate	West	TEC-PH-910	Xerox 1986	$ 13.36	2	0	$ 6.41	$ -
6/1/2021	Priority Delive	6/2/2021	CK-12205	Chloris Kastensmid	Consumer	South	FUR-BO-332	KI Conference Tables	$ 129.89	6	0.2	$ 12.99	$ 25.98
7/1/2021	Standard Freig	7/10/2021	BD-11620	Brian DeCherney	Consumer	South	TEC-PH-911	Eldon 200 Class Desk Accessories	$ 310.69	7	0.2	$ 108.74	$ 62.14
8/1/2021	Priority Delive	8/2/2021	MH-17785	Maya Herman	Corporate	West	FUR-BO-333	Avery Fluorescent Highlighters	$ 567.12	10	0.2	$ (28.36)	$ 113.42
9/1/2021	First Class	9/4/2021	PS-18970	Paul Stevenson	Home Offic	West	TEC-PH-912	Office Star - Swivel Chair	$ 187.76	4	0	$ 76.98	$ -
10/1/2021	Priority Delive	10/2/2021	TG-21640	Trudy Glocke	Consumer	South	FUR-BO-334	Metal Folding Chairs	$ 1,125.49	7	0.2	$ 98.48	$ 225.10
11/1/2021	Priority Delive	11/2/2021	VM-21835	Vivian Mathis	Consumer	Central	TEC-PH-913	Innergie Charging Kit	$ 16.28	2	0	$ 6.51	$ -

Figure 10.2: Excel Table with a new column.

SubTotal function

When a Total row is added to the Table, the calculation in the formula bar displays as SUBTOTAL.
To check this, click on *Total of Profit* on the Total Row. On the formula bar, the calculation will display as "=SUBTOTAL(109,[Profit])"
By default, in a Table all calculations are converted to SUBTOTAL.

Syntax:
SUBTOTAL(function_num,<column or range>)

Where:
function_num is a number 1-11 or 101-111 that denotes the function used for the subtotal and how it works with manually hidden rows and filtered rows.
1-11 includes manually-hidden rows (select rows, right-click and choose *Hide*), while 101-111 excludes them; filtered-out cells are always excluded.

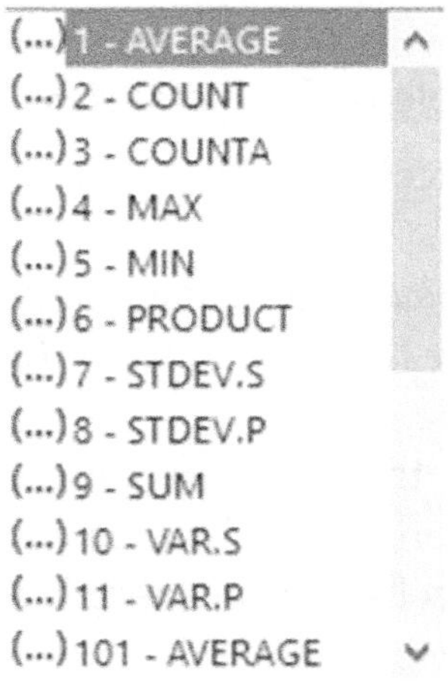

Figure 10.3: SubTotal function numbers.

The difference between SUBTOTAL and SUM is that SUBTOTAL ignores the filtered records, whereas SUM is calculated on all the rows including the hidden or filtered ones.

SUBTOTAL vs. SUM

The SUBTOTAL and SUM functions work differently when used in a calculation. The following exercise will illustrate the difference between the two functions.

Exercise2: Use the enclosed Chapter10.ExcelTable (Sheet SourceData) to perform this exercise.

- Convert the Source Data to an Excel table.
- Add a Table row to display the Total of Profit and Average of Sales.
- Check the difference between SUBTOTAL and SUM functions.

Refer to Chapter10.ExcelTable_Solutions.xlsx (Sheet Table2) for the solution.

Steps to create an Excel Table with a Total row:

1. Open Chapter10_ExcelTable.xlsx and navigate to the sheet named *SourceData.*
2. Make a copy of the *Source Data* sheet to preserve the original data for comparison. Rename the new sheet as *Table2.*
3. Create an Excel Table.
   - Select any cell within the data range. Go to the *Insert* tab in the ribbon and click on *Table.* The *Create Table* dialog will appear with the range of the cells pre-selected. Make sure to check the option *My table has headers.*
4. Add a Total row.
   - Click on any cell in the Table, and from the *Table Design* option in the ribbon, select *Total Row.*

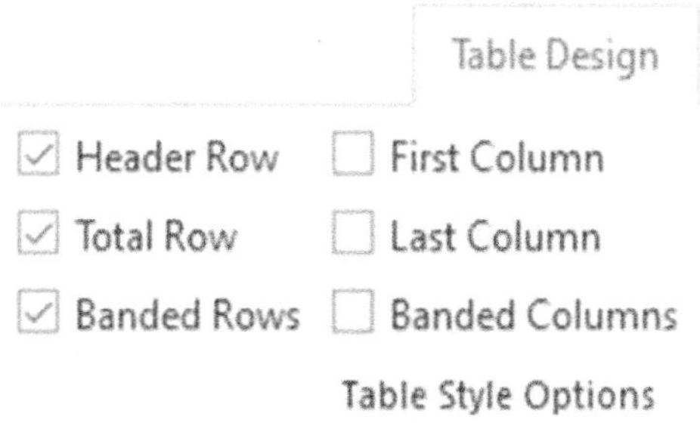

Figure 10.4: Total Row in the Table Design option.

This will display the *Total* label under the first column and *Total amount* under the last column, i.e., *Profit*.

Notice that a dropdown is displayed on every cell in the Total row, which shows different aggregation functions. Any function can be selected from the dropdown, and it will automatically perform the calculation.

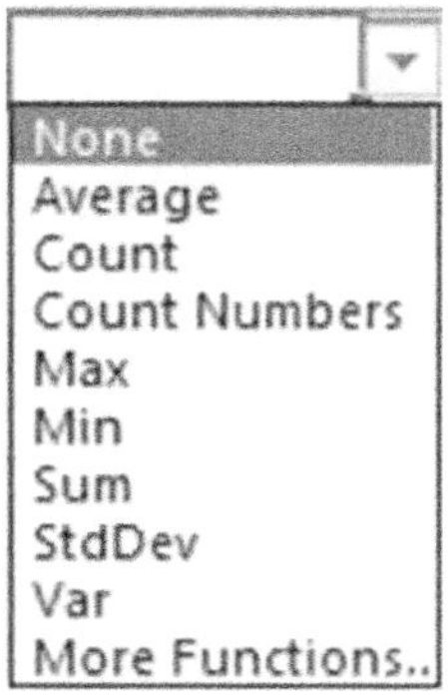

Figure 10.5: Aggregation options on the Total Row.

- Click on the Total row (Sales column) and from the drop-down, select *Average*. This will display the Average Sales.

5. SUBTOTAL vs. TOTAL
   a. Navigate to cell N14 and create the SUM (Profit) formula by typing =SUM (and selecting all the cells in the *Profit* column.

At this point, both SUBTOTAL and SUM will show the same amount as

$399.86

Now, filter the data on Region = Central.
The SUBTOTAL amount will change to $6.51, but the Sum will stay the same as $399.86.

Region	Product ID	Product Name	Sales	Quantity	Discount	Profit
Central	TEC-PH-913	Innergie Charging Kit	$ 16.28	2	0	$ 6.51
			$ 16.28			**$ 6.51**
					Sum of Profit	$ 399.86

Figure 10.6: SubTotal vs. Sum.

If the SUBTOTAL functionality is not desired, then use SUM.

Excel tables provide an efficient way to manage data. They are particularly useful when dealing with large datasets to perform data analysis. They offer added functionalities and features compared to regular data ranges, making data manipulation and calculations more convenient and efficient.

Chapter 11
Introduction to Excel Macros

The previous chapter provided an explanation of Excel Tables and how they can be used organize data in the worksheet. This chapter will focus on the usage of Excel Macros. Macros are powerful tool that automate repetitive tasks and enhance productivity. The chapter will delve into recording and running a macro, as well as exploring the VBA editor for editing and enhancing macro code.

The following topics will be discussed in this chapter:

- Overview of Macros
- Recording a Macro
- Editing the Visual Basic code for Macro

Overview of Macros

A Macro is a series of recorded or manually written commands that automate repetitive tasks within Excel.

- It comprises of set of instructions that perform a series of actions in a predefined order.
- Macros can be used to format cells, apply formulas, copy/paste data, generate reports, and more.
- They operate on a range of cells, so if new data or rows are added, the range of the Macro needs to be modified accordingly.
- Macros are recorded (specify set of instructions) and can be run to perform the actions specified in the instructions.
- Macro name should not have spaces in it.
- Macros are written in Visual Basic for Applications (VBA) code in the background.
- To save an Excel file with a Macro attached, it should be saved as an Excel Macro-Enabled Workbook (.XLSM).

- To access the Macro functionality, the *Developer* tab needs to be enabled in the ribbon. The Developer tab is not enabled by default and can be activated from the Excel *Options* menu.

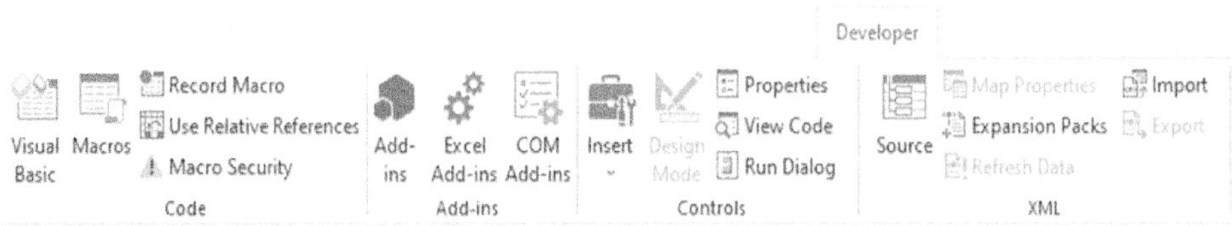

Figure 11.1: Developer tab to access the Macro functionality.

Enabling the Developer tab

Macros are created from the *Developer* tab in the ribbon, which is not enabled by default.

To enable the Developer tab:

1. Navigate to the *File* menu and go to More > Options.
2. In the *Excel Options* dialog box, select *Customize Ribbon* and check the option for *Developer* from the right.

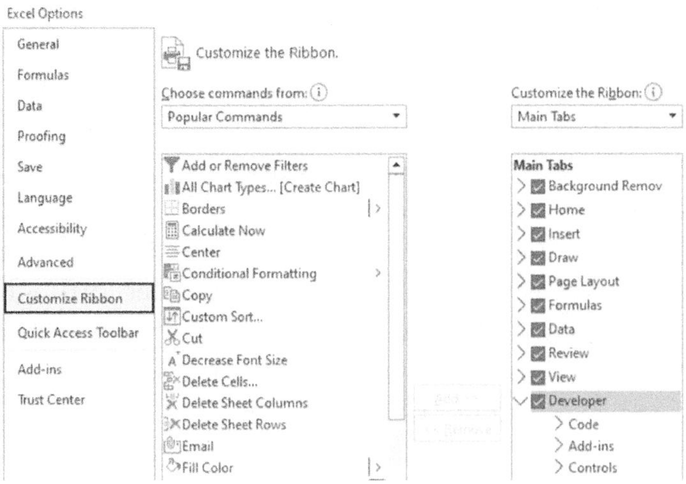

Figure 11.2: Enabling the Developer tab.

Enabling the *Developer* option in the Excel Options will display the Developer tab on the ribbon.

Recording a Macro

Macros are designed to automate repetitive tasks in Excel, saving time and effort for the user. The process of creating a macro involves three main steps: recording the macro, stopping the recording, and running the recorded macro.

The following exercise will create a macro to automate the formatting of data, which will streamline the formatting process and enhance productivity.

Exercise1: Use the enclosed Chapter11.IntroMacros (Sheet SourceData) to perform this exercise.

Write a Macro to automate the following tasks:

- Display negative Profit values in red color.
- Display Sales $500 in green.

Refer to Chapter11.IntroMacros_Solutions.xlsm (Sheet CreateMacro and Run Macro) for the solution.

Steps to create a Macro:

1. Open Chapter11_IntroMacros.xlsx and navigate to the sheet named *SourceData.*
2. Make a copy of the *Source Data* sheet to preserve the original sheet for comparison. Name the new sheet as Macro1.
3. Record/Create a Macro.
   - Navigate to the *Developer* tab in the ribbon and select *Record Macro.*
   - Provide the name of the Macro as Format_Sales_Profit.

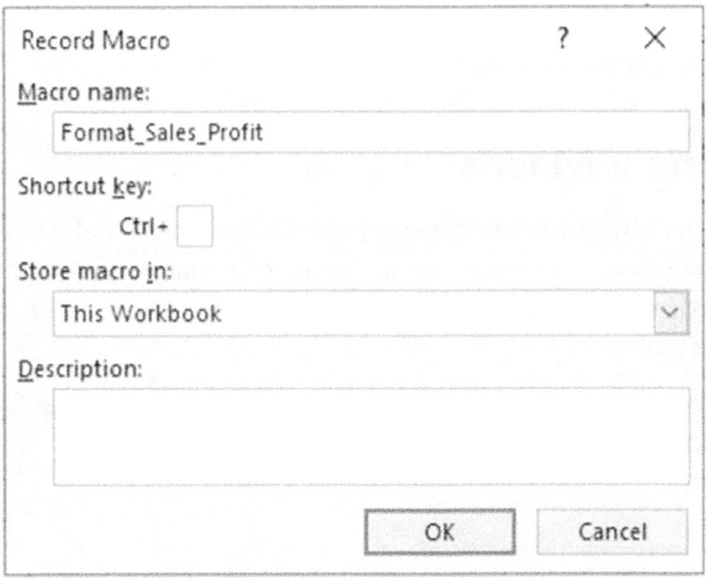

Figure 11.3: Recording a Macro.

- Perform conditional formatting to display Sales >500 in Green.
  Highlight the *Sales* column and navigate to *Home* > *Conditional formatting*.
  Select the option *Highlight Cells Rules* and choose *Greater Than*. Specify the condition as 500:

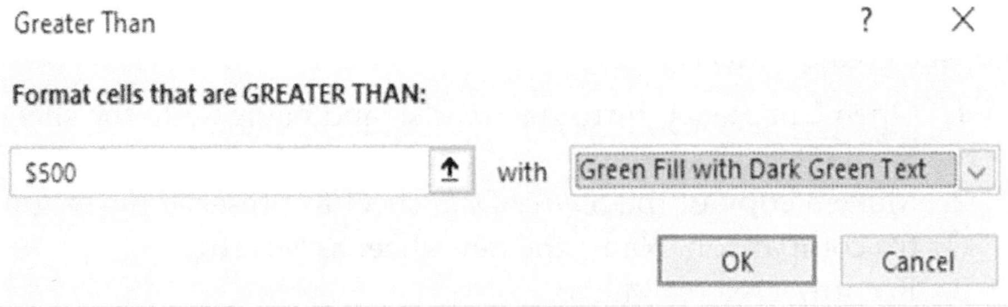

Figure 11.4: Conditional formatting for Sales greater than 500.

This will display the Sales greater than $500 in Green.

- Perform conditional formatting to display negative Profit in red.

Select the Profit column and navigate to *Home > Conditional formatting*.
Select the option *Highlight Cells Rules* and Choose *Less Than*. Specify the condition as:

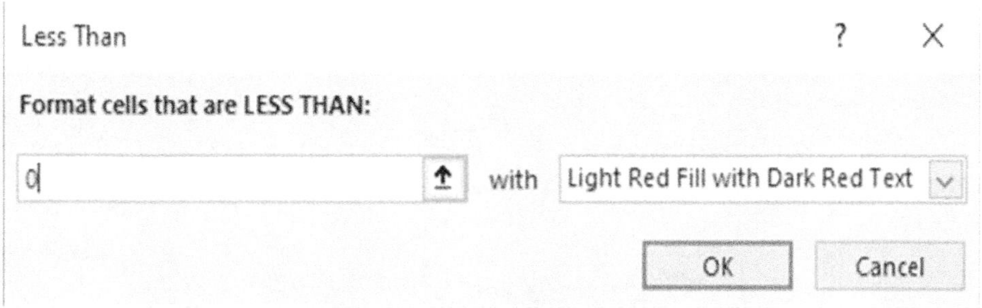

Figure 11.5: Profit less than 0.

This will display negative Profit in red color.

4. After completing the above tasks, navigate to the *Developer* tab in the ribbon and click on *Stop Recording*. This will stop the recording of the macro.
5. Run the macro.
    a. To observe the running of Macro, create another copy of the SourceData sheet and name it *RunMacro.*
    b. Navigate to the *Developer* tab and select *Macros*. The subsequent dialog will display all the Macros created so far. Select *Format_Sales_Profit* and click *Run*.

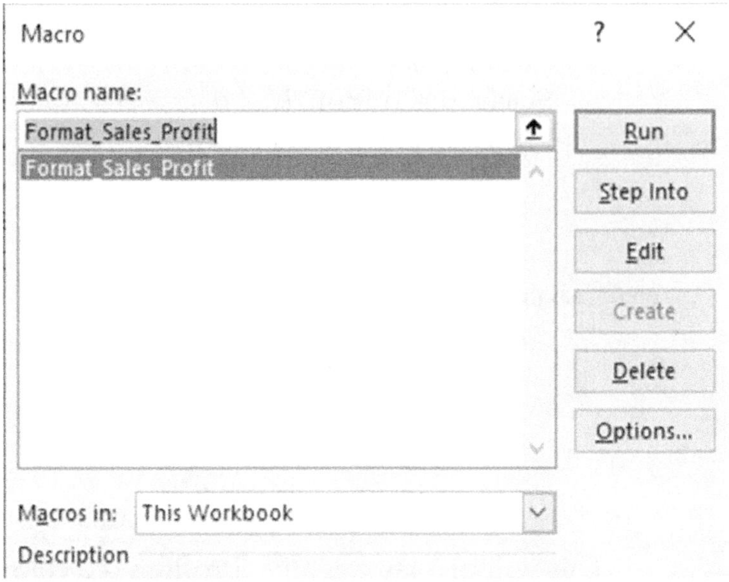

Figure 11.6: Executing the Macro.

This will execute the Macro and format the Sales and Profit columns as desired.

6. Save the file as an Excel Macro-Enabled Workbook (.XLSM) so that the Macro remains attached to it. Save the file as Chapter11.IntroMacros_Solutions.xslm.

How Macro will help

In the previous exercise, a Macro named Format_Sales_Profit was created to automate the formatting of the Sales and Profit columns. Now, whenever a similar file is received, the macro can be run to apply the desired formatting. This helps save time and ensures consistency in data formatting across different files.

- To observe this, create a new Excel file that contains same data as Sourcedata.
- Navigate to the *Developer* tab and select *Macros*. The subsequent dialog provides the option to select a Macro recorded in a different xlsm file. In our case, it is

- Chapter11.IntroMacros_Solutions.xlsm. It also shows the name of the Macro - Format_Sales_Profit.

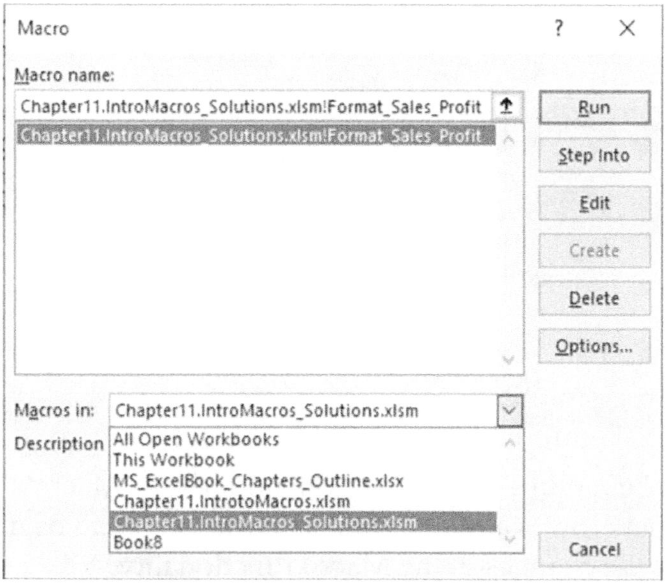

Figure 11.7: Running Macro on a different Excel file.

Select the correct file and click on *Run*. It will change the formatting of Sales and Profit as specified in the Macro with no action required from the user.

Visual basic code for Macros

Macro creates a Visual basic code in the background, which is useful to enhance the Macro functionality.

To access the code, follow these steps:

Open the XLSM file where the Macro was recorded.

Go to the *Developer* tab, and click on the *Visual Basic* option. The code will appear in a new window:

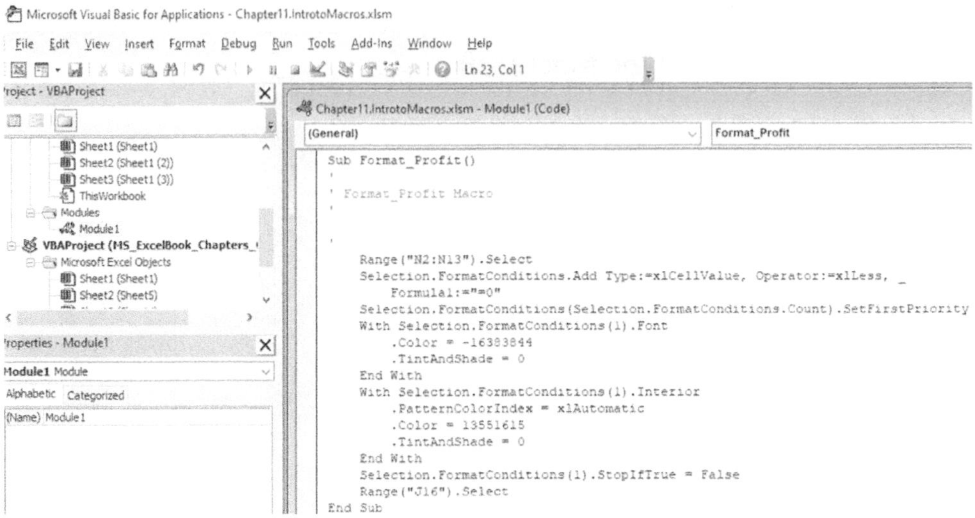

Figure 11.8: Visual Basic code for a Macro.

This code can be modified to change the underlying Macro's behavior. For example, if a new row is added to the data, the range can be updated in this code to reflect the changes in the Macro functionality.

Excel macros are sets of recorded or manually written commands that automate repetitive tasks in Excel. Excel macros are a powerful tool to simplify complex tasks, automate repetitive actions, and maintain consistency in data formatting and processing across different files.

Index

M

P

R

S

T

W

Made in United States
North Haven, CT
01 March 2025

66249429R10096